Politics in Japan: From Tradition to Challenge
Politics in France: From Protest to Politics, and
Politics in the Soviet Union: From Ideology to Orthodoxy
Politics in the United States: From Radical to Reason
Politics in West Germany: From Division to Unity

About the Series

Politics in [series text]... the contrast between
the two main theoretical perspectives, each title
examines the [politics]... [and the] change of the
primary institutions... and is concerned to
reach developmental...

POLITICS IN CHINA

FROM MAO TO DENG

About the Series

Chambers Political Spotlights aim to provide a bridge between
conventional textbooks and contemporary reporting. Each title
examines the key political, economic and social changes of the
country, providing, in addition, a brief contextual background to
each development discussed.

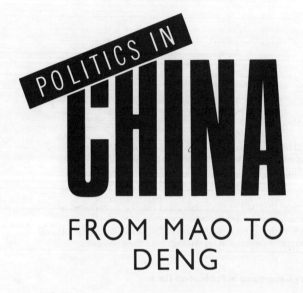

FROM MAO TO DENG

Ian Derbyshire
Ph.D. Cantab

Chambers

First published by Sandpiper Publishing as a Sandpiper Compact, 1986
This edition published by W & R Chambers Ltd. 1987
Reprinted 1988

British Library Cataloguing in Publication Data

Derbyshire, Ian
    Politics in China: from Mao to
    Deng.—(Chambers political spotlights).
    1. China—Politics and government—1976-
    I. Title
    320.951   JQ1502

    ISBN 0-550-20743-0

Typeset by Bookworm Typesetting Limited, 9a Gayfield Square, Edinburgh
Printed in Great Britain at the University Press, Cambridge

Acknowledgements

This book is based on a wide range of contemporary sources including
*The Times, The Guardian, The Independent, The Observer, The Sunday
Times, The Economist, Newsweek, Time, Keesing's Contemporary
Archives, The Annual Register* and *Europa: A World Survey*.

Every effort has been made to trace copyright holders, but if any have
inadvertently been overlooked the publishers will be pleased to make the
necessary arrangements at the first opportunity.

Contents

Preface

The years after 1972 saw Mao Zedong and his able, but age-ing, lieutenant Zhou Enlai set about reconstructing China's shattered political system after the chaos of the 'Cultural Revolution'. They were opposed in this work, however, by the ultra-leftist 'Gang of Four' led by Mao's wife, Jiang Qing.

Zhou and Mao finally died in 1976 and a violent succession struggle ensued involving the 'Gang of Four' and a group of Zhouist modernisers led by the elderly Deng Xiaoping. Neither side emerged victorious at first and, instead, Hua Guofeng, a moderate and loyal Maoist, was elected as the CPC's stop-gap leader. Hua proceeded to order the arrest of the 'Gang of Four' and dominated Chinese politics for twenty-seven months.

Hua's authority was, however, progressively challenged by Deng, who, after expanding his power base, finally emerged as de-facto leader of the country after the 3rd Plenum of the 11th CPC Central Committee in December 1978. Deng proceeded to dominate Chinese affairs during the following eight years and radically remodelled its political and economic system, establishing in power a new generation of leaders, effecting a proper balance between the state, party and military, and embarking upon a path of 'market social-ism' in agriculture and industry.

This Spotlight examines the key changes in the Chinese political and economic system during the years between 1972 and 1987. It looks at the changing functions of political institutions, at factional struggles within the CPC, at the modernisation programmes of Zhou and Deng and at changes in China's foreign policy.

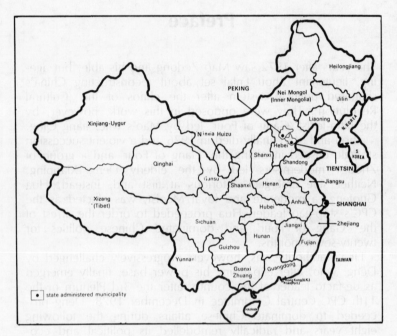

FIGURE 1: The Provinces of China

• state administered municipality

Part One

THE CHINESE POLITICAL SYSTEM

Peasants, Mandarins and Emperors:
The Chinese Polity Before 1949

The political development of contemporary China has been influenced by three chief factors: the continued economic backwardness and poverty of what remains a predominantly agricultural nation; an inherited cultural system and social tradition which has stressed the virtues of corporatism and obedience rather than individualism and democracy; and the country's longstanding history and experience of unified and bureaucratic administration.

China, with an area of 3.7 million square miles, is equivalent in size to the United States, but boasts a population today in excess of one billion, a figure four and a half times that of America. This dense population, a quarter of the world's total, is crowded into the eastern third of the nation and the vast majority is employed in agricultural tillage. China remains ranked among the poorest nations in the world, with a GNP per capita of barely $330 per annum in 1985, one twentieth of the figure recorded by the Soviet Union and a fortieth of that of the United States.

During the period before 1600, by contrast, China was at the forefront of world culture and boasted the most advanced and sophisticated administrative and agricultural systems then visible. A unified empire, encompassing much of the area of present-day China, was established as early as 206 BC by the Han dynasty (206 BC-220 AD) which employed educated bureaucrats steeped in the ancient, secular thought of Confucianism. This philosophy stressed the importance of honour and virtue for the nation's rulers and of loyal and deferential respect for tradition, patriarchy and seniority among the general population. From the Tang dynasty (618-907 AD) onwards, these 'mandarin' bureaucrats were recruited through a competitive and open system of public examinations. They formed a scholar gentry élite which ruled the country in conjunction with a 'divine' emperor and powerful regional potentates in a relatively centralised manner. The stable and sophisticated political systems of the Tang and subsequent Song (960-1279) and Ming (1368-1644) dynasties provided a framework within which impressive technical and economic developments took place. Most notable was the construction of a large and advanced communications and irrigation network which criss-crossed eastern China, encouraged the outward extension of cultivation and raised agricultural yields, providing the basis for the tripling in size of the nation's population. It rose from a figure of 150 million in 1400 to 430 million in 1850, a figure equivalent to more than a third of the world's total.

This rapid increase in population served, however, to depress the 'economic surplus' and meant that little quantitative or qualitative increase in per capita national income was registered between 1400 and 1800. Lacking a stimulus to develop, few advances were made in the nation's industrial technologies and inward-looking China found itself falling progressively behind the West from the 18th century onwards. The country's final dynasty, the Manchu Qings (1644-1911), faced mounting internal rebellion, as population pressure increased, and was forced, following military defeats, to make humiliating Treaty Port concessions to Britain, France, Germany, Russia and Japan. A number of Chinese intellectuals, acutely aware of their country's relative decline, saw the need to learn from the industrialising West and to modernise both the nation's economy and its cultural system. However, they were to be blocked by reactionary forces grouped around the Dowager Empress Ci Xi, who dominated Imperial affairs between 1865 and 1889 and 1898 and 1908.[1] It was not until 1911, when the Manchu dynasty was finally overthrown by regional gentry and Western trained leaders of the New Model Armies in a republican revolution, that a genuine movement for reform began to emerge.

[1] The Chinese spellings in this narrative adhere principally to the modern *pinyin* (Chinese phonetic alphabet) style of romanisation, which replaced the traditional Wade-Giles system as the Chinese government's exclusive style of transliteration in January 1979. In the case of political figures most commonly known under the Wade-Giles system, the former style of transliteration is given in brackets. Exceptions are made for the cities of Canton, Peking, Tientsin and Nanking, which are referred to under the Wade-Giles system. It should also be noted that, under Chinese convention, surnames/family names precede Christian names.

From Revolution to Revolution: 1911 – 1949

The years between 1911 and 1949 were a time of inter-dynasty struggle which was finally resolved by the establishment of a Communist regime which, governed by its party-trained and educated élite, mirrored in a number of respects the preceding Confucian-based bureaucratic system. This inter-revolutionary period also saw a significant conflict between, and intermingling of, Chinese and Western philosophy and political thought which eventually resulted in the new regime grafting the concepts of Marxism-Leninism on to a novel political system.

Initially, the October 1911 revolution saw the installation of a modernising regime under the leadership of Dr Sun Zhongshan (Sun Yat-Sen). Sun, a Western-educated politician born near Guangzhou (Canton) in 1866, the son of a Christian-convert peasant farmer, gained strong support in the eastern and south-eastern seaboard cities which had long been open to Western influences. He aimed to establish a liberal, Western-style, moderately socialist democracy with an elected parliament and a codified legal system. He was opposed, however, by conservatives, drawn particularly from the more isolated north and west, led by the military commander Yuan Shikai, who was installed as president in March 1912 and proceeded to subvert the 1911 revolution's democratic reforms. Following Yuan's death in 1916, power devolved to regional military commanders during a decade which became known as the 'Warlord Period' (1916-26).

Sun Zhongshan retained significant authority in the Canton region of southern China during these years and established the *Guomindang* (Kuomintang — KMT) or Nationalist party. However, a growing number of Chinese intellectuals, anxious to recover the nation's lost pride and greatness, turned instead to communism, being deeply impressed by the Russian Revolution of October 1917 and by the new Soviet government's decision in 1919 to relinquish the Tsar's territorial concessions in China. A Chinese Communist Party (CPC) was thus founded in the French concession of Shanghai in July 1921, with a separate overseas branch (the Young Communist Party — YCP) being formed in Paris in June 1922 by students who included Zhou Enlai (Chou En-lai) and Deng Xiaoping (Teng Hsiao-p'ing).

The Guomindang and communists, encouraged by Moscow, worked closely together in south-east China's cities during the early 1920s and sought to reunify the country through a 'northern expedition' from Canton. This plan was implemented in 1926/7 and met with significant success, with the fertile Changjiang (Yangtze) valley, including the cities of Wuhan and Shanghai, rapidly falling to the Guomindang and communists. However, the death of Sun Zhongshan (March 1925), a year before this expedition commenced, meant that the Guomindang was now led by the Japanese-trained, military general Chiang Kai-shek (1887-1975), a conservative-minded man, who, with close links with businessmen, landlords and industrialists, abhorred the communists. Chiang thus staged a coup against the Communist Party in Shanghai in April 1927 and established his own right-wing Nationalist government in Nanjing (Nanking). He then proceeded to defeat the warlords of Beijing (Peking) and became the recognised head of China's central government. Chiang's actions forced the communists into hiding in the rural hinterland of the south and it was here that they developed a distinctive new form of communism.

China's early communists were divided into three groupings during the 1920s. On one wing there were the Shanghai and Canton-based intellectuals led by Chen Duxiu, the head of the Chinese Communist Party until 1927, Li Lisan (party boss 1927-30) and Wang Ming, who were well versed in the theoretical works of Marx and Lenin and who enjoyed close contacts with the Russian Communist Party and its Comintern (Communist International) agents. They favoured an urban and industrial trade-unionist led revolution, adhered closely to the orthodox Moscow line and retained firm control over the CPC executive until 1935. On the other wing stood, Mao Zedong (Mao Tse-tung: 1893-1976), a middle peasant's son from rural Hunan province, whose educational attainments and reading of communist literature were less impressive. Mao had served as a library assistant at Peking University and taught as a headmaster in Changsha but was more an intuitive communist who believed, heretically, that in agricultural China revolution would emanate from the countryside as poor peasants rose up in revolt against the oppression of their gentry landlords. A third group, the sophisticated Paris-trained 'work study' intellectuals led by Zhou Enlai, bridged these two wings and worked with whichever was the more dominant.[1]

---

[1] The 'work-study' scheme had been devised by Chinese and French educational officials to enable bright Chinese students, who had passed special examinations and who could provide 200 silver dollars for the travel expenses, to take a 1 – 2-year course in Paris free of all tuition fees on the condition that they devoted part of their time to factory work in the labour-short French economy.

The forced flight of the communists into the countryside from 1927 strengthened the Maoist wing of the party. In the inaccessible mountain stronghold of Jingganghshan on the Hunan-Jiangxi border, Mao Zedong began to devise a unique brand of rural-based Third World communism. He initially introduced fair rents and a measure of land reform and established genuine public support for his People's Red Army by ensuring that his troops dealt fairly with local citizens, paying proper prices for articles taken or used. He then, in combination with his military commander Zhu De (Chu Teh), devised an effective system of mobile guerrilla warfare, based to a large degree on the ancient and popular Chinese texts of the 'Water Margin' and Sun Tzu's 'Art of War'. Mao's position within the Chinese Communist Party was strengthened after 1931 when the Moscow-dominated underground party in Shanghai, whose strategy of fomenting urban-based revolution had patently failed, was purged in the 'White Terror' by Chiang Kai-shek and forced to flee to Jiangxi. From this period on, Mao's strategy of building up popular support in rural *soviets* (workers' republics) and establishing politically motivated guerrilla units was to form the basis of Chinese communism.

In the short term, however, Mao's Jiangxi soviet had to encounter the growing military threat posed by Chiang Kai-shek's one million strong, German-trained, KMT forces. During 1932 Chiang had launched a 'Bandit Encirclement Campaign' with the aim of exterminating the CPC's rural soviets in central China one by one. By the autumn of 1932 he had liquidated He Long's Hunan-Hobei soviet and had forced the evacuation of the large Oyuwan soviet (located on the borders of Hunan, Henan and Anhui) and during 1933 began to impose an economic and military blockade of the Jiangxi soviet. Faced with the alternatives of surrender or starvation, the CPC leadership at Jiangxi decided to concentrate their forces, break out from Jiangxi and head on a zig-zag north-westerly course towards isolated Shaanxi in northern China in what became known as the 'Long March' of 1934-36. During this march Mao, a natural leader who had been pushed into the sidelines between 1932-35, established his ascendancy within the CPC and wrested executive power away from the dominant Shanghai-based Moscow faction. He was elected party chairman at the Zunyi conference in February 1935, having gained the support of Zhou Enlai, who had formerly been allied with the Moscow faction. The 'Long March' was an epic journey covering 6000 miles of harsh, often mountainous, terrain in twelve months and involved more than 100 000 men, women and children. It represented a desperate retreat from the Guomindang forces and resulted in casualty losses in excess of 85%. By 1936, however, the Red Army had reached the safe haven of Yanan in northern Shaanxi with 1000 of its original force and 30 000 men and women in all. The party had survived, and had become battle hardened; it had spread its message throughout the countryside and had developed a strong leadership grouping composed of figures who were to dominate Chinese politics during the half century ahead.

At Yanan Mao and the Communist Party established a new base in the north of the country and rapidly built up popular support among the oppressed peasants of Shaanxi province. Mao formed a new 'people's republic', rebuilt the Red Army and began studying and formulating his own new communist theories. The period in Yanan was important in establishing northern support for what had previously been a predominantly southern-based Communist Party. Yanan was, however, of even greater significance, being adjacent to Dongbei (Manchuria),which had been annexed by Japan in 1931. This enabled Mao, a fervent nationalist by nature, to declare war on Japan and call on Chiang Kai-shek to end his 'Extermination Campaign' against the communists and join instead in a united front against the foreign enemy. Chiang initially rejected this offer, but was forced into a humiliating climb-down in December 1936 following the mutiny of former Manchurian troops at Xian, the capital of Shaanxi province. The internal civil war was finally halted and the autonomous communist 'border state' around Yanan was recognised as the CPC gained new respectability.

Within seven months, following the Japanese storming of Peking, the Guomindang-Communist pact came into operation and the war between China and Japan commenced. The conventional and urban-based forces of Chiang Kai-shek were rapidly overwhelmed by the Japanese, who captured Tianjin (Tientsin), Nanking and the Yangtze valley. Chiang's gentry-led troops were eventually driven into hiding in remote Sichuan province in the far west of the country. The Red Army, by contrast, fought an effective mobile and rural-based guerrilla campaign and proved difficult for the Japanese forces to pin down and defeat.[1] They retained control of hinterland areas in a large swathe of northern China stretching across Hebei, Shanxi, Shandong,

---

[1] During this period the Red Army was divided into two groupings: the Eighth Route Army, centred in the north, led by Zhu De and comprising 30 000 troops in 1937 and the 10 000-strong New Fourth Army, based in the south-east and led by Ye Ting.

Shaanxi and Henan provinces and emerged as popular 'freedom fighters', whose just treatment of the local population contrasted starkly with the brutality of the Japanese forces. After 1942 Japan's attention became diverted by American and Allied troops elsewhere in Asia, so the CPC's control of north-central China deepened and the Red Army expanded, with the new recruits being inculcated with the teachings of Marx, Lenin and Mao.

When the war with Japan ended in August 1945, Chiang Kai-shek was rapidly airlifted by the American airforce to take control over Manchuria, which had briefly been held by Russian troops. He declared himself head of the Chinese government; however, he was faced with tremendous economic problems and with mounting communist opposition during a civil war which commenced during the early summer of 1946. The burgeoning Red Army (now renamed the People's Liberation Army) cut Chiang's supply lines, before decisively defeating the 550 000-strong Guomindang forces at the battle of Huai-Hai in December 1948. Chiang fled to Taiwan and on 1 October 1949 the People's Republic of China was proclaimed. The nation's 40-year succession crisis was over as this new regime became firmly established with a distinctive ideology and system of organisation.

Communist China: Political Organisation and Philosophy

Communist China's political system replicates in many respects the Soviet Union model. It functions as a one-party state, dominated by the Communist Party of China (CPC), which represents the vanguard of the working class and the guardian of a revolution which had taken place, contrary to Marxist tenets, in a backward, almost feudal, nation.[2] The CPC provides policy ideas and leadership and oversees the work of the state channel of government. Its members are disciplined and controlled from the top downwards through the system of 'democratic centralism'.

[1] Eight minor parties — the China Association for Promoting Democracy (chairman, Ye Shengtao), the China Democratic League (chairman, Hu Yuzhi), the China Democratic National Construction Association (chairman, Hu Juewen), the China Zhi Gong Dang (chairman, Huang Dingchen), the Chinese Peasants' and Workers' Democratic Party (chairman, Ji Fang), the Guomindang Revolutionary Committee (chairman, Zhu Yunshan), the Jiu San Society (chairman, Xu Deheng) and the Taiwan Democratic Self-Government League (chairman, Su Ziheng) — are allowed to operate in communist China, but they have no real influence or role in the political system.

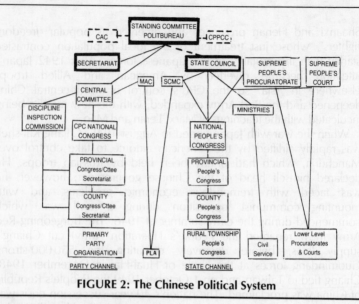

FIGURE 2: The Chinese Political System

The Party Hierarchy and Machine

Membership of the CPC has expanded from barely 0.3 million in 1934 to 1.2 million in 1945, 4.5 million in 1949, 17 million in 1961 and 44 million today — a figure which represents 4% of the total population.[1] Each member is carefully selected, following recommendation by at least two serving party workers, and serves a probationary period which includes dutiful study of the teachings of Marx, Lenin and Mao.[2] Members, once fully accepted, then rise by seniority to positions of leadership (*cadres*) in a slow, almost Confucian, fashion.

The party is organised hierarchically and constructed in the shape of a huge pyramid. At the lowest level are the basic units, or Primary Party Organisations (PPOs), which are set up in every farming community, factory, office, school and army unit where there are three or more party members. Their tasks consist of implementing

[1]   This contrasts with a figure of 6.5% of the total population for the Communist Party of the Soviet Union (CPSU).

[2]   Membership of the CPC is invariably preceded by a period in the Communist Youth League (YCL), an organisation open to those between the ages of 15 and 25, which presently boasts 48.5 million members and is headed by Song Defu. The YCL, in addition, supervises the work of the Young Pioneers, a body for children between the ages of 9 and 15 which operates in schools and has a membership of 50 million.

the decisions of higher party bodies, 'guiding and supervising' workplace units, passing on upwards reactions to party directives and increasing ideological awareness among ordinary workers. They act as the eyes, mouth and ears of the CPC at the local level.

Above the PPOs, CPC organisation units are to be found at the prefecture, district/county, municipality, provincial, autonomous region and national levels (see Figure 2) and operate along classic Leninist 'democratic centralist' lines. Under this system, policies are supposed to be frankly and democratically debated during their formulation stage, but must then be implemented with disciplined obedience once they have been agreed upon. This system, also, entails the subordination of lower level units to superior bodies, which pass on orders which must be dutifully followed and which determine the membership of organisations below through a system of 'recommended elections'.[1]

Party Congresses are elected at the county (*xian*) level triennially and at the province (*sheng*), autonomous region and autonomous municipality levels at five-yearly intervals. Real authority rests, however, with the smaller party committees, standing committees and secretariats which are selected, following guidance from above, by these congresses. The First Secretaries who head the standing committees in the country's 21 provinces and three autonomous municipalities are particularly powerful individuals, acting as important links and 'brokers' between the localities and the centre.[2]

The National Party Congress is the highest organ of the CPC. Members are elected by a series of indirect delegate conferences up the different rungs of the party ladder. The congress is in theory elected every five years. In practice, however, terms have varied. The Congress met six times between 1921 and 1928, three times during the next 41 years (in 1945, 1956 and 1969) and a further three times (in 1973, 1977 and 1982) in the period after 1969 (see Appendix B). The National Party Congress is, on paper, a most powerful organ which is supposed to elect the party's Central Committee and

---

[1] Under 'democratic centralism' the formation of factions is strictly forbidden and minorities are expected to accede to the superior wisdom of the majority. Since 1982, however, provision has been made within the new party rules (see articles 14-16) for individuals to refer matters for a second opinion to the next party level, though in the meantime they must continue implementing the agreed decision.

[2] A list of China's provinces and autonomous municipalities (that is municipalities subordinate only to the central government) is given in Appendix A.

approve policy and organisational changes. In reality, however, this large 1500-2000-member body meets only for a few days each quinquennium and is primarily a showpiece. The decisions it takes have already been recommended and approved by superior executive organs, before being passed on for its unanimous ratification. Congress is thus concerned primarily with generating enthusiasm and favourable publicity for the CPC and is used by the party leadership for signalling and ratifying important and symbolic changes in direction

It is in the three apical executive bodies of the party, the Central Committee, the Politbureau and the Secretariat, that real power resides in Communist China.

The Central Committee, which is 'elected' by the party Congress, has (at present) 210 full and 133 alternate (non-voting) members. It meets in plenary session at least twice a year and is filled with the élite cadres of the CPC. The members are elderly (with an average age of 66 years in 1980) and 90% male-dominated, despite the post-Confucian drive towards sex equality. They include military and state government · officers, intellectuals, trade union and youth league officials, as well as provincial and prominent municipal and county level party secretaries. The Central Committee has a number of functional departments of its own, but its primary task is to 'elect' the Politbureau and to ratify policy decisions.

It is the 20-25-member Politbureau which is the key formation in Communist China. It functions as a quasi-cabinet in day-to-day charge of the country, meeting once a week. It is composed of elderly, experienced and committed party members, who occupy uppermost positions of responsibility not just within the party but also in the state government and in the military. There are always a number of varying personal and ideological groupings inside the Politbureau and the grouping which commands a majority is able to dictate party policy and control subordinate appointments, including those to the Central Committee.[1]

Within the Politbureau there is also an 'inner cabinet' or Standing Committee comprising five leading party figures — the CPC General Secretary (the party's official head: see Table 1), the Prime Minister, the State President and the chairmen of the MAC and CCID — which exerts overarching authority. An important adjunct

[1] In communist China such factional groupings are termed *shan-tou* ('mountain-tops') and are invariably based around shared historical ties (service in the same army or region) and involve patron-client relationships between senior leaders and their protégés.

to the Politbureau is the twelve-member and functionally divided Secretariat, operating under the direction of the CPC's General-Secretary. It provides administrative back-up and co-ordinative support and takes a key role in the detailed formulation of new policies and the vetting of personnel for party, state, military and diplomatic posts.

TABLE 1 : Leaders of the CPC since 1949

	Year of Birth	Term as Leader
Mao Zedong[1]	1893	Feb 1935 — Sept 1976
Hua Guofeng[1]	1920	Sept 1976 — June 1981
Hu Yaobang[2]	1915	June 1981 — Jan 1987
Zhao Ziyang[3]	1919	Jan 1987 —

[1] Party Chairman
[2] Party Chairman June 1981 — Sept 1982. Party General-Secretary Sept 1982 — Jan 1987.
[3] Party General-Secretary

Three other bodies have important powers. The 132-person Central Commission for Inspecting Discipline (CCID) ensures that party rules are adhered to, maintains a watch over ideology and supervises the work of similar provincial and county commissions below it. The five-member Military Affairs Commission (MAC) exerts strong party control over the Chinese army (PLA) and oversees a network of political commissars. Finally, the recently formed 172-member Central Advisory Commission (CAC), set up in 1982, functions as a general consultative body and is composed of senior and retired party, state and military figures.[1]

The State Hierarchy

Although the party cadres dominate policy in Communist China, there is, as in the Soviet Union, a parallel state system of government which is in charge of the more routine work of administration and which gives a gloss of legitimacy to the whole

[1] Members of the CAC must have at least 40 years' party standing and are elected by the CPC Central Committee for a concurrent term. The CAC elects its own smaller 24-member Standing Committee which is headed by a chairman who must also be a member of the Politbureau Standing Committee. Members of the CAC are entitled to attend CPC Central Committee plenary meetings as non-voting participants and vice-chairmen of the CAC may also attend Politbureau meetings in a similar capacity.

political system. This state hierarchy closely mirrors the party hierarchy, but it is the latter that oversees, dominates and controls the state bodies. There is, in addition, an intermixing and intertwining of the two branches of government, with senior party personnel staffing many prominent state posts of responsibility (see Figure 3), although recently there has been an attempt to foster a clearer separation between the channels.

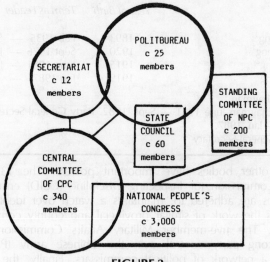

FIGURE 3:
State Government and Party Interconnections

At the lowest level of the state hierarchy, the small town and rural township, citizens over the age of 18 vote directly for candidates for local People's Congresses at three-yearly intervals.[1] They used to vote openly through a show of hands and select from lists of party-approved candidates, the number of whom corresponded exactly with the number of deputies required. Elected candidates then went on to vote by secret ballot for deputies to be sent to higher level congresses and ultimately to the National People's Congress. Recently, however, particularly since 1979, the state system has become somewhat more open and democratic. Voting by secret ballot has been extended downwards to the local level, while direct elections have been extended upwards to the county

[1] The term of office for People's Congresses above county level is five years.

rung. In addition, elections have become more competitive: the number of candidates standing now exceeds the number of places available by 50 — 100% at the base level and by 20 — 50% at higher levels and nominations are more open to all groups.

The congress at each level of the state system elects a smaller People's Council Standing Committee from a slate of names presented by the party committee. This council meets every two to four weeks and carries out day-to-day administration and is functionally divided into departments from the county level and above. It is predominantly party staffed and follows orders from both superior state councils and from party committees at its own level.

The indirectly elected National People's Congress (NPC) is, in theory, the legislature or parliament for the People's Republic of China and the highest organ of power. Elected every five years or less and packed with around 3000 delegates, it now meets once a year for a period of one to two weeks to ratify economic plans and constitutional changes and to 'elect' the Republic's President (a ceremonial post), Vice-President, Prime Minister and State Council members.[1] (See Tables 2 and 3 for lists of the PRC's Presidents and Prime Ministers.) In reality, however, the NPC is a 'rubber stamp' body which follows the wishes of the CPC executive. More powerful is its smaller Standing Committee of 133 members at present, which meets fortnightly and supervises the conduct of elections for the NPC, interprets laws, oversees the work of the State Council, appoints key judicial officers and enacts legislation by decree in specified spheres in between sessions of the NPC. Half of its members are key party officers.[2]

Even more important is the State Council, an administrative cabinet which is composed of 33 departmental ministers, nine heads of commissions, eleven State Councillors (a number of whom are also prominent departmental ministers), the Secretary-General, the Auditor-General, the President of the People's Bank of China, five Vice-Premiers and, at its head, the Prime Minister (Premier). This Council represents the leading executive body in

[1]   For dates of election of past NPCs see Appendix B.

[2]   Included in the NPC Standing Committee are representatives of minority nationalities, but the committee itself is dominated by an inner core composed of a chairman, 19 vice-chairmen and a secretary-general. (See Appendix C for the composition of this grouping in 1986). Under the 1982 constitution, the Standing Committee's members are debarred from holding any post in the administrative, judicial or procuratorial organs of the state.

the state government, overseeing the departmental and administrative apparatus, in charge of day-to-day management of the country and empowered to submit new policy proposals to the NPC or its Standing Committee. It meets once a month with an 'inner cabinet' of 18 (comprising the Prime Minister, Vice-Premiers, State Councillors and Secretary-General) which meets more frequently.[1] It is filled almost fully with CPC Central Committee members.

TABLE 2 : Presidents (Heads of State) of the People's Republic of China

		Term in Office		
Mao Zedong[1]	Oct 1949	—	April 1959
Liu Shaoqi[2]	Apr 1959	—	Oct 1968
Dong Biwu[3]	Oct 1968	—	Jan 1975
Zhu De[4]	Jan 1975	—	July 1976
Sung Qingling[5]	July 1976	—	Mar 1978
Ye Jianying[4]	Mar 1978	—	June 1983
Li Xiannian[6]	June 1983	—	

[1] Chairman of CPPCC and Chinese People's Government Council (CPGC) 1949-54, Chairman of PRC 1954-59.
[2] Chairman of PRC
[3] Acting (Deputy) Chairman of PRC
[4] Chairman of NPC's Standing Committee
[5] Acting (Deputy) Chairman of NPC's Standing Committee
[6] President of the PRC

TABLE 3 : Prime Ministers of the People's Republic of China

	Year of Birth	Term in Office		
Zhou Enlai	1898	Oct 1949	—	Jan 1976
Hua Guofeng	1920	Jan 1976	—	Sept 1980
Zhao Ziyang	1919	Sept 1980	—	

Outside the formal elected state channel of authority is the Chinese People's Political Consultative Conference (CPPCC), a broad-front advisory body which includes technocrats, intellect-

[1] Under article 87 of the 1982 state constitution, the Prime Minister, Vice-Premiers and State Councillors are restricted to two consecutive terms in office. For the most recent composition of the State Council and its inner cabinet see Appendix C.

uals and overseas Chinese. It met regularly between 1949-64 and has been revived in recent years in an attempt to give a wider base to the Chinese polity.

The state sphere of government also includes the judiciary, headed by the Supreme People's Court and the Supreme People's Procuratorate (SPP), a body which supervises lower level Procuratorates, sanctioning arrests and trials, and which functions as a state prosecutor in a manner similar to the American District Attorney. A regularised and codified criminal legal system has been established in recent years and operates in an unusually public manner, mixing together Chinese tradition and Western practices. Major restrictions are still, however, placed on unconstitutional 'anti-party' activity, while the CPC's committees and political departments wield considerable judicial influence.

The People's Liberation Army

The third pillar of the modern Chinese polity is the 3-4 million strong People's Liberation Army. The PLA played a crucial role in the victory of the CPC in the years between 1934 and 1949 and was a body in which all China's elderly leaders served either as commanders or as political commissars, and it has retained political significance during the decades after 1949. With its well trained, educated and ideologically indoctrinated personnel, the PLA has provided considerable assistance in mobilisation and reconstruction drives. The PLA, along with the reserve militia, also played a prominent political role during the 'Cultural Revolution' and, under the leadership of Lin Biao, acquired great authority, almost running the country through the military-dominated 'revolutionary committees'. However, the PLA, described by Mao as the 'Great Wall of China', has always obeyed the party, which has retained firm control over the 'barrel of the gun'. In recent years the political power of the army has been reduced significantly as the CPC leadership has sought to turn the PLA into a more specialised and professional body on the Soviet Red Army model.[1]

---

[1] The CPC exerts political and ideological control over the PLA through the MAC, which works in conjunction with the PLA's Political Department and is linked to its lower levels through a chain of political commissars. The state looks after the PLA's professional concerns through the defence ministry and the State Central Military Commission (SCMC), a body which is appointed by the NPC.

The 'Sinification' of Communism

The brief exposition above demonstrates the close similarities between the Chinese and Russian political systems. There are, however, striking and important differences.

The most basic is the unitary, single chamber nature of the Chinese polity compared to the federal and bicameral structure of the Soviet Union (USSR) with its Chamber of Nationalities. This has reflected the greater homogeneity of China which, despite its vast population and visible north-south and east-west differences, encompasses less than half the area of the USSR and 94% of its people are Han-Chinese, suffused with a common Confucian, Buddhist and Taoist culture.[1] This contrasts with the ethnic, religious and linguistic diversity and cleavages between the European, Muscovite and Central Asian regions of the Soviet Union.

Another important difference is the continuing predominance of peasants and the rural sector in underdeveloped Communist China. In 1980 69% of the Chinese labour force was employed in agriculture, while only 19% worked in industry and 21% lived in towns. In the Soviet Union, at the same date, only 14% was employed in agriculture, while 45% worked in industry and 63% lived in urban areas. The Chinese Communist Party has thus remained more rural-based, with more than half its members being drawn from the peasant community, although during recent years emphasis has been placed upon recruiting skilled, usually urban, technocrats.

The size and importance of this rural sector has, however, created considerable practical and philosophical problems for the CPC leadership and has resulted in its pursuing, since the mid 1960s, a unique mixed agricultural and industrial development strategy.

According to Marx's original theories, communist revolutions were only meant to occur in the developed and industrialised West where a 'bourgeois mode of production'· was in place. Marx believed that in these countries the contradictions in capitalism would lead to an uprising by the exploited factory proletariat who

[1] There are five autonomous regions, Xinjiang-Uyghur (population 13.4 million), Nei Monggol (Inner Mongolia, population 19.8 million), Xizang (Tibet, population 2 million), Guangxi-Zhuang (population 38 million) and Ningxia-Hui (population 4 million) on the mountainous periphery of China and 56 recognised 'minority peoples'. (See Appendix A for the administrative divisions of China).

would go on to establish a truly classless society. Such revolutions had failed, however, to occur by 1900 and the industrial worker in the West, instead of becoming progressively poorer, had increased in affluence. This persuaded Lenin to modify Marx's thought to add the concept of imperialist 'super-profit', whereby the capitalists of the West were exploiting the backward periphery to such a degree that they were able to raise wages at home and mollify the industrial proletariat. Lenin thus saw the need for a series of revolutions in the world's periphery to bring down the global imperial system and precipitate a final cataclysm in the advanced nations. These peripheral revolutions were to be led by disciplined and enlightened communist parties in combination with the nascent urban proletariat, with the peasantry being used only as a background force.

Mao, the dominant figure in Chinese politics between 1935 and 1976, drew much from the writings of Marx and Lenin, but he also made allowances for Chinese circumstances and for his own practical experience. He created the unique and eclectic 'sinified' philosophy of Marxism-Leninism-Maoism. This philosophy broke away from orthodox Marxism-Leninism on a number of important points.

Firstly, victory in the Chinese revolution was achieved through the triple alliance of a disciplined party and army working in combination with the peasantry. The urban proletariat played only a limited role and it was significant that the post-1949 Chinese polity was not termed a 'dictatorship of the proletariat', as in the Soviet Union, but was termed a 'government of the four classes — the proletariat, peasantry, petty bourgeoisie and national bourgeoisie'. There were attempts during the initial post-revolution years to concentrate recruitment among the urban proletariat but this did not last long. Mao, a coarse and earthy countryman who felt ill at ease among sophisticated townsmen, sought to ensure that the simple virtues of rural life were not lost. He gave unusual emphasis to the rural sector in his economic plans and sought to restrict the development of wide rural-urban differences through the launch of periodic 'rustication campaigns' in which urban-educated youths and party cadres were despatched to the countryside to engage in manual labour and live alongside peasants.

Secondly, Mao placed great emphasis on man's inherent rationality and malleability. He believed that people could be taught to see the errors of their ways and viewed the communist revolution as one not just of economic but also ideological change

17

in which people's ways of thinking would be slowly transformed. Great emphasis was placed upon indoctrinating party members with correct teachings and upon educating the new republic's citizens, particularly the peasantry, in an effort to achieve full communism within a lifetime. Reactionary and 'counter-revolutionary' groups, including landlords and the bourgeoisie, were subjected to thorough 're-education' sessions, as were party members who stepped out of line.

Thirdly, Mao was aware of the danger that under the communist state a new party élite would arise, presiding over a new form of 'state capitalism'. Thus he was vigilant against the emergence of bureaucratism and privilege and saw the need for a regular series of 'rectification campaigns' (*zhengfeng*) to keep the élite on their toes. The most dramatic of such campaigns was the mid 1960s 'Great Proletarian Cultural Revolution'. This failed to achieve its ambitious aims and instead rapidly got out of hand, creating chaos and often unjust victimisation. What is true, however, is that Mao's 'perpetual revolutions' prevented the Chinese communist system becoming as ossified as that of the Soviet Union. Chinese communism remains more decentralised and democratic in structure, with greater opportunities being available for the recall and criticism of cadres.

Mao's influence remains substantial in Communist China today. There has always, however, been considerable debate between different policy approaches and between different leadership figures as the pages which follow demonstrate. Since 1978 there has been a significant reaction against Maoist thought as a new post-Mao leadership grouping has assumed power.

Part Two

POLITICAL DEVELOPMENTS SINCE 1949

Instability and Change in Communist China: 1949 – 1972

The political history of Communist China during the four decades since 1949 has been one of instability. There have been frequent factional struggles within the party élite which have led to a series of sudden policy shifts as well as changes in the varying strength of different institutions within the Chinese polity.

The factional divisions evident within the CPC during the 1920s and 1930s (see page 4) persisted after 1949, though in an altered form. One grouping within the party still favoured orthodox urban and industrial-based development and remained sympathetic to Moscow. It included the Manchuria and Eastern Region party chiefs Gao Gang and Rao Shushi, who were both purged in February 1954, the PLA commander and later Minister of Defence, Peng Dehuai, and the man who rose to become briefly head of state, Liu Shaoqi. Occasionally allied to this group was a second faction on the 'right' and 'centre-right' of the party comprising Deng Xiaoping and allied urban and former 'work study' intellectuals. They favoured a pragmatic approach to economic development, utilising education to create a pool of skilled technocrats, the modernisation and professionalisation of the armed forces, the establishment of a balanced party-state political system based around a collective form of leadership and a codified body of laws and civil rights. The gradualist premier Zhou Enlai was sympathetic to the aims of this group. On the left of the CPC was the third faction, the 'Maoists', led by the party chairman himself and supported by his security chief, Kang Sheng, his political secretary, Chen Boda, and the radical young followers of his fourth wife Jiang Qing. They sought to remove rank distinctions from the PLA, pay differentials from industry and private plots from agriculture in a truly classless, egalitarian fashion. In addition, they placed emphasis on the need

19

for ideological reform, under the slogan 'better red than expert', in an effort to achieve full communism within their leader's lifetime.

United Front Reconstruction: 1949-1956

The years immediately following the communist takeover in 1949 were directed towards the reconstruction of a nation and an economy which had been torn asunder by more than a decade of internal strife and warfare. Party chairman Mao Zedong and his CPC colleagues sought co-operation in this vast effort from intellectuals and technocrats at home and from the Soviet Union outside, in what represented a continuing socialist 'united front'. During this period, order was gradually restored, the dismembered communications network swiftly repaired, a Soviet-influenced 'heavy industry first' Five Year Economic Plan (1953-57) adopted and a moderate and popular programme of land reform introduced. The latter measure dispossessed large landlords, the backbone of the KMT, and redistributed land in tiny plots to small tenants and the landless.

Those dispossessed were tried and forced to repent. The two to four million who refused were executed. Politically, these 'reconstruction years' saw the convening of a broadly-based Chinese People's Political Consultative Conference (CPPCC), which included representatives of party, religious, ethnic and interest groups, to elect a 56-member Chinese People's Government Council (CPGC). Headed by Mao Zedong, this council assumed provisional executive, legislative and judicial control over the country, before the PRC's first constitution was adopted by the NPC in September 1954. In addition, the period between 1949-56 saw the recruitment and training of six million new members by the CPC, with special emphasis being placed on the enrolment of industrial workers and educated groups. Party membership rose to 10.7 million. This period was concluded by the convening of the 8th CPC Congress in September 1956, the first such meeting for eleven years. A new party Central Committee and powerful Politbureau were elected, and also a detailed new party constitution was framed which stressed the principle of collective leadership.[1]

In retrospect the first six years of communist rule in the PRC were

[1] The CPC Politbureau elected at the 8th CPC Congress comprised 17 figures: Mao Zedong, Liu Shaoqi, Zhou Enlai, Zhu De, Chen Yun, Deng Xiaoping, Peng Dehuai, Lin Biao, Lin Bochu, Dong Biwu, Peng Zhen, Luo Ronghuan, Chen Yi, Li Fuchun, Liu Bocheng, He Long and Li Xiannian.

unusually successful. The nation was pacified and unified and proved capable of expelling United Nations (predominantly American) troops from North Korea during the Korean War of 1950-3. The economy was rebuilt, with industrial production rising by 18% per annum and agricultural output by 4.5% per annum. Finally, a new party-state political system was created and commenced functioning in a smooth and balanced fashion.

The Failed Leap Forward: 1957-1965

During the years after 1956, however, divisions began to emerge between the left and right wings of the CPC over future strategy in what later became termed the 'two-lined struggle'. The party's right wing, which included Prime Minister Zhou Enlai, commerce minister Chen Yun and party vice-chairman Liu Shaoqi, favoured adhering largely to the 1949-56 policy approach and proposed making only slight adjustments in the Second Five Year Plan (1958-62) with the aim of giving greater emphasis to light consumer industry production, raising material incentives at the local factory level and devolving a number of planning powers to the regional authorities. By contrast, Mao and the party's left wing were less content with the record of the First Five Year Plan period. They felt that during these years agricultural growth and investment had been allowed to lag seriously behind that of industry, that the economic system had become too centralised and bureaucratic and that regional and income differentials had seriously widened, causing the re-emergence of new class conflicts. The Maoist 'left faction' thus proposed major new reform initiatives designed to counteract these 'counter-socialist' tendencies.

To deal with the growing agricultural problem, Mao Zedong began to encourage a switch away from small-scale private plot farming towards large-scale co-operative, 'pooled farming', a policy shift which became established when all boundary marks were eliminated from fields in 1956. To rouse the bureaucracy, Mao, gaining the initial support of Zhou Enlai, launched the 'Hundred Flowers Campaign' during 1956-57, in which intellectuals were encouraged to openly criticise the incumbent regime and make suggestions for improvements.[1] This was followed in 1958 by the introduction of the radical economic programme termed the 'Great Leap Forward' which aimed to achieve rapid growth in both the industrial and agricultural production at the same time — the policy

[1] This campaign soon got out of hand, resulting in excessive criticism of party cadres, and had to be brought to a close in June 1957.

of 'walking on two legs'. The programme sought to combine centralisation with local initiative and the use of both large-scale modern factory technologies and small-scale traditional 'intermediate technologies'. Above all, however, it entailed the creation of huge, almost county-size, self-sufficient agricultural communes which would grow foodstuffs, manufacture tools, consumer and industrial items and function as local political units and communist 'education' centres. These communes, it was hoped, would bring to an end the traditional divide between town and country and would foster the creation of a new breed of 'complete communists' who combined the Maoist virtues of both mental and manual labour.

The 'Great Leap Forward' was a radical and ambitious scheme which broke sharply away from the Soviet model of development. In retrospect, however, it proved to be a sad failure and was an ill-judged example of attempting to 'run before walking'. Firstly, it proved impossible for the state and party bureaucracy to co-ordinate efficiently local and national level initiatives as production became centred in the new, largely autonomous, communes. There was a tremendous waste of scarce resources, with blockages developing on the burdened railway network and factories being forced to shut down production as a result of periodic shortages of spare parts and raw materials. Secondly, in the countryside, the peasantry, being used to a more individualistic form of agriculture, resisted the shift from private plots to communes as well as direction by imported party cadres, often ignorant of local agricultural practices and farming conditions, and who propagated a new communalistic form of living. Thirdly, matters were seriously compounded by an unfortunate series of floods and famines between 1959-62 followed by the withdrawal of Soviet technical aid in August 1960 as a result of the widening rift in Sino-Soviet relations. Thus, although output did initially increase during 1958, production in both the industrial and agricultural sectors slumped dramatically between 1959-61, causing serious food shortages and resulting in the death from starvation and ill-health of more than 20 million people during the period of the 'Great Leap' experiment.

The failure of the 'Great Leap Forward' led to criticism of Mao Zedong and the emergence of a challenge to his leadership. Particularly outspoken was the defence minister, Peng Dehuai, the son of a Hunanese peasant and an old Jiangxi Soviet and 'Long March' colleague of the party chairman. Peng had emerged as a popular military hero following his successful command of China's troops during the Korean war. He favoured the creation of a modernised, professional and élitist army and party machine and opposed the impending break with the Soviet Union and Mao's rash communalisation programme. He presented a deeply critical 'Letter of Opinion' at the July-August 1959 Lushan plenum of the CPC Central Committee in which he clearly set out these views. 'Rightist' colleagues failed, however, to support Peng after Mao threatened to resign and return to the countryside to lead a new Liberation Army to establish true communism. Instead, Peng found himself being denounced as 'anti-party' and was placed under house arrest and replaced by the radical Lin Biao as defence minister.[1] This episode displayed the continued strength of support for Mao Zedong within the CPC Central Committee during a period of relative weakness. It also highlighted the force of Mao's charismatic personality and his willingness to go outside the party itself and appeal to the broad masses for support in a populist, 'Caesarian' manner.

More serious opposition to the party chairman came from Liu Shaoqi (1898-1969), another Hunanese peasant's son who had attended the same local college as Mao Zedong. Despite these common roots, however, Mao and Liu emerged as starkly different figures. Liu, who later studied in Moscow in 1921/2 and worked as an underground labour organiser in the Nationalist controlled 'White Areas' during the later 1920s, developed into a coolly calculating Russian-style *apparatchik* and became the second-ranking officer in the CPC. He favoured a more traditional and cautious urban-industrial economic strategy under the direction of a hierarchically organised and tightly controlled communist party and placed economic development ahead of social and ideological change in his list of policy priorities.

Liu, who had previously served as CPC General-Secretary at the head of the party Secretariat between 1945-56 and as Chairman of the NPC's Standing Committee between 1954-58,replaced Mao as President (Chairman) of the People's Republic in April 1959. He then proceeded to implement a centrist 'recovery programme' between 1960-64 which sought to remove the worst excesses of the 'Great Leap Forward', restore political stability and achieve renewed economic growth. Working with the CPC's new General-Secretary, Deng Xiaoping, Liu began to break up and reduce communes in

[1]   Peng died in prison in 1974.

size, brought an end to the use of communal mess halls and dormitories, enhanced the role of local agronomists, increased agriculture's share of total investment and sanctioned the reintroduction of small, private subsidiary plots and the use of rural markets. Decentralisation and material incentives were also extended to industry in a programme which proved to be remarkably successful.

This 'recovery programme' led once more, however, to a widening of income differentials and the recrudescence of bureaucratic élitism. It was seen as dangerously 'revisionist' by Mao Zedong, who feared the re-emergence of a new class system and the overthrow of the 1949 revolution, just as the French and Russian revolutions had been subverted. He viewed Liu (who was later to be termed 'China's Khrushchev'), Deng and other senior leaders as seeking to 'take the capitalist road' through encouraging private aggrandisement and selfish profit-seeking. The austere party chairman was particularly vexed to hear Deng declare in a famous statement, 'Private farming is all right as long as it raises production, just as it does not matter whether a cat is black or white as long as it is a good mouser'. Such an emphasis on ends rather than means conflicted sharply with Mao's own philosophy which saw the need for the hand-in-hand development of a selfless and egalitarian communist outlook, even if this was at the expense of a faster rate of economic growth — the policy of 'putting politics in command'.

Mao Zedong, forced away from centre stage since 1960, saw the need to oust Liu, Deng and other 'capitalist roaders' and at the same time launch a major 'rectification campaign' with the aim of radically fashioning popular attitudes. He set about preparing this dramatic counter-strike during the early 1960s, beginning first by building up support among younger elements of the PLA who, under the guidance of Lin Biao, had been since 1960 progressively inculcated with Mao's teachings, in the form of the pocket-sized *Little Red Book*. During the autumn of 1962, the party leader launched the Socialist Education Movement (SEM), another 'rectification campaign' aimed at rooting out cadre corruption and eliminating movements towards the recrudescence of capitalism. The SEM sought, in addition, to restore idealism in Chinese politics and was targeted towards lower-middle peasant organisations and students, who now became subjected to the party leader's radical writings.

Mao Zedong's Cultural Revolution: 1966-1971

The Socialist Education Movement which continued throughout 1963 and 1964 was the precursor to a more far-reaching 'rectification campaign' which shook Chinese society during the years between 1966-69 and had ramifications throughout the period up to 1976. 'The Great Proletarian Cultural Revolution' proved to be a complex and extended struggle which formed in many ways a second, but less successful, revolution. At its simplest level, the 'Cultural Revolution' began as a power struggle between Mao Zedong and Liu Shaoqi, the effective leader of the country between 1962-65, and it developed, following Liu's fall, into a further series of power struggles between Mao, ultra-leftist radicals and Lin Biao. On a second level, the 'Cultural Revolution' represented an attempt radically to transform public and political attitudes in a progressive manner. Finally, on a third level, it represented an attempt by Mao to nurture a new, younger and radicalised generation of party leaders who would be in a position to take over power after his death. It thus took on the outward appearance in many respects of a clash between the young and old and between established cadres and the rank and file.

Liu Shaoqi attempted initially to retain firm party control over the Socialist Education Movement 'rectification campaign' by leaving it to higher level cadres to scrutinise the behaviour of junior party members and to draw attention to their errors. Mao, by contrast, sought broader popular participation, with ordinary peasants investigating cadre corruption in a 'mass line' and from-the-bottom-up approach. Liu's attempts to muzzle the Socialist Education Movement finally persuaded Mao to move directly to oust the State President and fellow 'capitalist roaders' by unleashing his newly radicalised student and PLA supporters. The first stage in this process was the release of the 'Twenty-Three Points' by the Central Work Conference in January 1965 which stated that the struggle between socialism and capitalism was evident within the party itself, with some of the CPC's leaders seeking to 'take the capitalist road'. Mao approved of this document and called for a Cultural Revolution to eradicate the 'bourgeois mentality'. At first this movement was confined to the academic and cultural sphere, before moving directly into the political arena in May 1966 with the release by the CPC Central Committee of Mao's 'May 16 Circular' which stated that a number of bourgeois 'counter-revolutionary revisionists' had infiltrated the party, government and army leadership and were seeking to overthrow the revolution. Mao called on the masses to liberate themselves and a series of wallposter campaigns began, directed against Liuist leaders.

Young 15-19 years old Red Guard students, radicalised by the SEM campaign, acted as Mao's early shock troops in 1966. One million were transported to Peking to root out 'reactionary and bourgeois' party leaders. Their main targets were Liu Shaoqi, Deng Xiaoping, Peng Zhen (Mayor of Peking and a Politbureau member), Marshal He Long, Lu Dingyi (Minister of Information) and the modernising army chief-of-staff, General Luo Ruiqing, each of whom was gradually forced out of office and paraded around the streets wearing a dunce's cap. The movement was directed by Mao, Kang Sheng (chief of the secret police), Chen Boda (editor-in-chief of the Central Committee's theoretical journal 'Red Flag'), Jiang Qing and Lin Biao, with Premier Zhou Enlai providing grudging support and attempting to act as a moderating influence. However it rapidly got out of hand, as the Red Guards sought to uncover further 'bourgeois reactionaries' hiding within the middle and lower levels of the party apparatus. Bitter power struggles developed all over China in provincial and county towns, with old scores being settled, as the country descended during 1966/7 into a confusing state of anarchy which shattered the party-state political and judicial machine that had functioned smoothly between 1954 and 1965.

The most radical departure occurred in Shanghai where the Liuist party committee was overthrown in January 1967 and a commune on the 1871 Paris model was established by Zhang Chunqiao, Yao Wenyuan and Wang Hongwen, members, together with Jiang Qing, of the notorious, ultra-leftist 'Gang of Four'. Similarly, at the rural level, a number of communes were also taken over by radicals who proceeded to introduce extreme communalistic land policies. In general, however, such was the confusion during 1967 that the PLA had to be called in to restore order, reassert central authority and deal with the anarchic ultra-leftist 'Young Generals'. By July 1968 this had largely been achieved. The Red Guards had been dispersed into the countryside to 'learn from the peasants' and a tripartite system of government established in the form of the new provincial 'Three Part Revolutionary Committees', comprising Maoist party cadres, trade union leaders and army commanders. The chair on these committees was invariably held by a military officer, enabling the PLA to exert *de facto* control over the country during 1968/9 in what was a sad end to Mao's utopian revolutionary vision.

By 1969 the radical phase of the 'Cultural Revolution' was over and there was a gradual return to a more settled form of government, signalled by the holding of the 9th CPC Congress in Peking in April 1969. This Congress, which was notable for the large number of new faces attending and elected to the party's ruling councils, went on to approve a new party constitution.[1] It removed Liu Shaoqi from his position as head of state and expelled him from the party, recognised Lin Biao as the party chairman's 'chosen successor' and made the thoughts and writings of Mao Zedong once again central to the functioning of the Chinese polity.[2] In addition, the Congress elected a new Politbureau Standing Committee, comprising Mao Zedong, Lin Biao, Chen Boda, Kang Sheng and Zhou Enlai, to assume control of party and national affairs.

The 9th Congress's moves towards political reconstruction were, however, only halting and partial. Strong divisions remained evident in a Congress which lasted for the unusually lengthy period of 24 days. On the one extreme, ultra-leftist Red Guard radicals, supported by Chen Boda (the former head of the 'Cultural Revolution Group'), wanted to incorporate a number of the innovations of 1966/7 into a new and more democratic political system based on the Paris Commune model. A second and more powerful group, comprising Lin Biao and the PLA, who provided two-thirds of the Congress members and half of its Central Committee and Politbureau, sought to retain the power they had gained in 1967/8 and to introduce a strong presidential form of government with the ultimate aim of making Lin Biao China's sole ruler. A third group, centred around the pragmatic and moderate State Premier, Zhou Enlai, rejected any radical new departures and wished only to return to a settled party-state system of the form which had operated before 1966. The latter grouping gained the support of Chairman Mao, who had become disillusioned with the anarchic activities of the young radicals during 1966-68 and who now sought to restore and re-establish a sound economy.

Mao therefore set in train moves to weaken and purge Chen Boda and Lin Biao, forcing the pair into a desperate alliance in an effort to depose the party chairman and install Lin as President. Mao gained prior knowledge of this scheme and had it blocked at the CPC Central Committee meeting held at Lushan (Jiangxi province) in

---

[1] 80% of the new 279-member (170 full) Central Committee were freshmen and 64% of the new 25-member (21 full) Politbureau.

[2] Liu died in November 1969, having been locked away in a disused bank vault in Kaifeng (Henan province).

August 1970, on which date Chen Boda was dismissed from the party. Lin Biao (1908-71), the talented and ascetic Wuhanese-born commander who enjoyed significant support within the PLA, proved more difficult to oust. A great flatterer of the party chairman and his wife Jiang Qing, he appeared still to be outwardly loyal. He was, however, a neurotic and ambitious man, who may have been working in secret alliance with the Soviet Union. In 1971, with his health rapidly deteriorating, Lin formulated 'Project 571' with the intention of assassinating Chairman Mao during a train journey between Shanghai and Peking and assuming power following a military coup. However, the plot was uncovered and Lin, forced into hasty flight towards the Soviet Union in an inadequately fuelled plane, died when his aircraft crashed in Outer Mongolia in September 1971. This extraordinary episode removed the last significant opponent to Chairman Mao and brought down the final curtain on the controversial 'Cultural Revolution'.

The Reconstruction of the Party-State System: 1972-1975

The years after 1972 saw the uneasy balancing of power between the left and right, radical and moderate, wings of the CPC and the slow reconstruction of the pre-1965 party-state political system. This system had been almost completely shattered by the Cultural Revolution. Many key institutions, including the Secretariat (which had been a power base for party Secretary-General Deng Xiaoping and had included Peng Zhen, Lu Dingyi and Luo Ruiqing) and the NPC, had fallen into disuse. The legal system had been made ruthless and arbitrary and the state bureaucracy, party and Politbureau had been denuded of personnel through 'rightist' purges as power had gravitated into the hands of Mao, Lin Biao and the young radicals.

The political instability of 1966-71 naturally had an adverse effect on China's economy and it was clear in 1972 that, just as after the 'Great Leap', a period of order and stability was now required. Mao, recognising this, now stepped back from day-to-day administration and allowed Prime Minister Zhou Enlai to set about the reconstruction of the nation.

Zhou had acted as the steady tillerman at the helm of China's state bureaucracy throughout the post-revolution years. He had worked in close partnership with party chairman Mao Zedong, although differing substantially in both character and outlook. Zhou, born in

March 1898 in Huaian near Shanghai, came from an urban, mandarin gentry family and enjoyed an extensive education, studying up to degree level in Japan and Paris. He emerged as a sophisticated, well read, internationally-minded and practical intellectual, in contrast to the crude, coarse and insular visionary-philosopher, Mao Zedong. He enjoyed a happy and stable family life with his wife Deng Yingchao, a friend since youth, in contrast to the unhappy, four times married, party chairman. He had been, in addition, an adherent to the CPC Moscow line before 1935 and emerged later as a supporter of a balanced, 'centre-right' technocrat approach to economic development, utilising material incentives, in opposition to radical, communalistic Maoism.

However, despite these differences, a powerful bond of friendship developed between Zhou and Mao. Zhou, coming from an impoverished family in decline which had seen better days, shared with Mao a fervent commitment to the communist ideal and the personal attributes of frugality and thrift. Having been rejected by his parents at birth and been brought up by his uncles, he was an insecure man who placed great value on fidelity in personal relations. Once he had decided to side with Mao at the crucial February 1935 Zunyi conference, he remained implacably loyal during the next 40 years and content with his subordinate position as State Premier. Although not always seeing eye to eye with the party chairman, he never sought to form a rival leadership faction and continued to support Mao even through the excesses of the 'Cultural Revolution'. In return, Zhou was protected from damaging criticism during the radical poster campaigns of 1967/8 and was allowed to continue his efficient superintendence of the administrative machine.

After 1972, as the ageing Mao retired more and more from public affairs, Zhou slowly set about rebuilding the state bureaucracy and economy. He gradually restored many of the experienced and skilled cadres who had been purged between 1966-68 and reintroduced private plots and material incentives to encourage agriculture and industry. He brought the PLA under firm party control and began to refashion a strong collective CPC leadership which would be in a position to assume power peacefully once he and Mao finally departed to 'meet Marx'.

The first evidence of this reconstruction was to be found in 1972 and early 1973 with the rehabilitation of 20 senior military commanders who had been purged during 1966-9, the sacking of 250 radical pro-Lin officers, and the reinstatement of a clutch of powerful 'rightist' party technocrats, including Li Xiannian (finance minister), Ye Jianying (defence minister) and Deng Xiaoping, as well as Zhu De and Dong Biwu.[1] Party recruitment drives were also stepped up, with CPC membership rising by possibly 8 million to 28 million between 1969 and 1973, while congresses were once again convened for the Communist Youth League, trade unions and, finally, the CPC in 1973.

The 10th CPC Congress, which met for five days in August 1973, represented in many respects the real beginning of a return to order and normalcy. A further substantial number of purged cadres returned to the Central Committee (totalling 22% of the committee's new intake); the PLA's representation fell dramatically from 46% to 23%; and an effective new Politbureau and Standing Committee was now elected. (See Table 4.) However, power was still clearly divided between the centre-right and the radical left of the party grouped around the Shanghai-based 'Gang of Four', all of whose members enjoyed seats in the Politbureau.

The key figure in the 'Gang of Four' was Mao Zedong's controversial wife, Jiang Qing (1913-), the daughter of a brutal Shandong carpenter and his estranged servant wife, who began life as a Shanghai actress and was briefly married during her teens. She later met and entranced Mao Zedong when he was based at Yanan in 1937 and they were married in 1939. Following her marriage, Jiang began immersing herself in communist literature and was given charge of cultural affairs in 1960. She emerged as radical, puritanical and egalitarian in outlook, although enjoying a great personal love of material luxuries. Her power and influence grew progressively. During the early 1960s and between 1966 and 1969 she worked with Chen Boda at the head of the 'Cultural Revolution Group', the body charged with directing the Cultural Revolution, and formed the powerful 'Gang of Four' faction with three younger Shanghai politicians — Zhang Chunqiao (55, a former writer and local party leader), Yao Wenyuan (49, another radical writer) and Wang Hongwen (38, a former textile mill worker).

The 'Gang of Four' remained powerful during 1973, with Wang Hongwen occupying number three ranking position in the CPC Standing Committee, after Mao and Zhou, and appearing destined

---

[1] Li Xiannian, Ye Jianying, Zhu De and Dong Biwu, unlike Deng Xiaoping, had not been publicly dismissed and purged during the 'Cultural Revolution'. They had, however, lost influence, being ignored and bypassed as administration was effected instead by the new PLA-dominated Revolutionary Committees and Military Councils.

TABLE 4: The CPC Politbureau and Standing Committee in August 1973

Standing Committee

Mao Zedong (CPC Chairman)	Wang Hongwen[1]
Zhou Enlai (State Premier)	Zhang Chunqiao[1]
Ye Jianying (Defence Minister)	Kang Sheng (Security Chief)
Zhu De (MAC)	Dong Biwu (Dpty. Head of State)
Li Disheng (PLA Cmdr. NE Region)	

Remainder of Politbureau

Wei Guoqing	Secr. Guangxi Prov. Pty Cttee
Chen Yongkui	Secr. Shanxi Prov. Pty Cttee
Yao Wenyuan[1]	2nd Secr. Shanghai Pty Cttee
Ji Dengkui	Secr. Henan Prov. Pty Cttee
Hua Guofeng	Secr. Hunan Prov. Pty Cttee
Wang Donxiang	Dir. C Cttee Gen. Office
Jiang Qing[1]	Culture Minister
Liu Bocheng	A former Marshal
Li Xiannian	Vice Premier
Wu De	Secr. Peking Pty. Cttee
Xu Shiyou	Cmdr Nanking Region
Chen Xilian	Cmdr Shenyang Region

[1]Members of the 'Gang of Four'

to assume the party leadership once Chairman Mao departed. The 'Gang' also controlled the media and party propaganda machine and had direct access to Mao himself. They were anxious to ensure that a radical political course was adhered to and they formulated, with Mao's support, a series of new 'rectification campaigns'. The most important was the anti-Confucius campaign, which, launched during the autumn of 1973, encouraged criticism of the ancient sage for his reactionary views on patriarchies, hierarchies and the role of women. The 'Gang' hoped to broaden this campaign into a broader attack on what they saw as the 'reactionary' policies of the Zhou administration, that had reintroduced the use of examinations in schools (abolished in 1966) for streaming pupils in an élitist, technocratic manner and which was downgrading the importance of ideology and manual labour in the assessment of official personnel. Zhou, however, managed to deflect this criticism by coupling the anti-Confucius campaign with attacks on Lin Biao and by emphasising that the political education and training of party members at rural cadre schools would remain an important priority. Eight million youths were sent for re-education in the countryside during 1974.

Zhou Enlai was, by 1973, a sick man. He had been told that he had incurable cancer and suffered two major heart attacks during 1974, forcing him into hospital from May onwards. Mao Zedong, four years Zhou's senior and afflicted with Parkinson's disease, was also visibly ailing. No clear arrangements had been made for his succession and, in consequence, a scarcely concealed succession struggle developed in the years after 1974.

Zhou Enlai sought during his final years to make further progress towards the re-establishment of a stable party-state system on the pre-1965 model. Firstly, with Mao's support, he reasserted firmer party control over the military by reshuffling the command of all eleven of China's military regions in the winter of 1973. This move, which brought to an end 15-20 years of regional control by a number of PLA commanders, was carried out in order to destroy local patronage networks and prevent the recrudescence of 'Red Warlordism' after the death of Mao and Zhou. In addition, Luo Ruiqing, the purged former chief-of-staff and Huangpu protégé of Zhou Enlai, was returned to high office in July 1975.

Secondly, Zhou endeavoured to establish Deng Xiaoping as his successor as State Premier. Deng, the country's 1st State Vice-Premier, took over Zhou's duties from the summer of 1974 and was appointed to the important post of chief-of-staff to the PLA in January 1975 and made a party vice-chairman and member of the CPC Politbureau's Standing Committee.

Thirdly, Zhou sought to gain effective sanction for the domestic reforms he had introduced since 1972 at the 4th National People's Congress which was called in January 1975, the first such congress to meet for eleven years. The Congress approved an amended state constitution, similar in many respects to that of 1954, and a new and balanced list of deputy premiers and state councillors.[1] It also, most importantly, saw Deng deliver Zhou Enlai's final report on the

---

[1] The 12 Deputy-Premiers appointed by the 4th NPC were: Deng Xiaoping, Zhang Chunqiao, Li Xiannian, Chen Xilian, Ji Dengkui, Hua Guofeng, Chen Yongkui (each being, in addition, a Politbureau member), Wu Guixian (a female textile worker from Shaanxi), Wang Chen (the former minister for state farms), Yu Qiuli (minister for state planning), Gu Mu (minister of construction) and Sun Zhian (a factory worker from Tientsin). In the new State Council, 60% of the ministers were veteran technocrat administrators with extensive pre-1966 ministerial experience.

economy in which he called for a new drive towards rapid economic growth under the title the 'Four Modernisations' (the modernisation of agriculture, industry, national defence and science and technology). This envisaged a two-stage programme with the aim of building 'an independent and relatively comprehensive industrial and economic system by 1980' and bringing the Chinese economy on a par with the West by the year 2000. It accepted, in addition, the right of citizens to enjoy, to a limited degree, ownership of their income, savings, home and other means of livelihood.

The radical 'Gang of Four' continued, however, to oppose the Zhouist development drive and instigated a further series of poster campaigns during 1974 and 1975. Those in May and June 1974 criticised supposedly corrupt and uncommitted party leaders, for example Wu De (the Mayor of Peking), and praised Wang Hongwen and Mao Zedong. The campaign of 1975, which was based around the slogans 'Study well the theory of the dictatorship of the proletariat' and 'Root out the bourgeois style of life', was launched directly by Mao Zedong, who had ostentatiously boycotted the NPC Congress.

Mao's views at this time were equivocal. He disliked the factional activities of the 'Gang of Four' and his relations with his ambitious and licentious wife, Jiang Qing, had become strained almost to the point of divorce. However, Mao's greatest fear was that the 'black cat, white cat' Deng Xiaoping would assume power and undo all he had stood for. He thus stirred up another bout of puritanical fervour, a small-scale 'Cultural Revolution', in 1975, with the launch of a major new campaign directed against privileges, bonuses and material incentives. This mass movement precipitated a series of disorderly strikes in Hangchow (Hangzhou) which had to be quelled by troops brought in by Deng Xiaoping in July 1975. Two months later Mao launched an even more direct attack on Deng himself. He called on the Chinese people to study the classic and popular novel *The Water Margin* and warned that a treacherous leader might, in the near future, try to assume power and attempt to reverse the socialist direction of the Chinese revolution. These 1975 campaigns were backed up by sinister moves by the 'Gang of Four'. One of its members, Zhang Chunqiao (chief political commissar of the PLA since January 1975), had begun overseeing the formation of radical people's militias in Shanghai and other major cities with the aim of staging a coup following Mao's death and installing himself as State Premier and Jiang Qing as party chairwoman.

1976 — The End of an Era?

The succession struggle shifted gear on 8 January 1976 when Zhou Enlai finally lost his fight against cancer and died in a Peking hospital. To general surprise, Deng Xiaoping, Zhou's natural successor, was passed over and the relatively unknown Hua Guofeng was publicly named as acting Premier on 7 February. Deng did read the eulogy at Zhou Enlai's funeral on 15 January, as requested by the former Prime Minister, but he rapidly became the focus of a series of virulent newspaper and university poster attacks and was forced to disappear from public view, along with his colleagues Ye Jianying and Li Xiannian. Deng, now being depicted as the chief bourgeois 'capitalist roader', was flown to the safety of southern China by his friend Xu Shiyou (military commander of the Guangdong region) and lay low while the 'Gang of Four' remained in the ascendant during February and March 1976.

Opposition to the 'Gang' became evident, however, during April 1976 when huge crowds assembled in Tienanmen Square in Peking to lay wreaths and pay homage to the immensely popular Zhou Enlai during the annual Qing Ming festival. The 'Gang', disturbed by this spontaneous display of popular feeling and the raising of banners critical of Jiang Qing and in support of Deng Xiaoping, decided to put a stop to the commemoration and removed the wreaths, poems and posters on 5 April. This only resulted, however, in larger and angrier demonstrations by more than 100 000 Zhou supporters and the eruption of a riot which had to be quelled by Peking militia forces, resulting in the injury or death of up to 10 000. Two days later, at a Politbureau meeting, Deng was blamed for the Tienanmen riot and was dismissed from his posts. He was allowed to retain his party membership on the wishes of Chairman Mao. The 'Gang of Four', now seemingly well established, spent the next four months attempting to win additional backing from senior ministers and officials to enable them to assume power peacefully after the ailing Chairman's death.

Mao eventually died on 9 September, two months after the ominous Tangshan earthquake, which was taken to herald the imminent end of a dynasty. His death, though not wholly unexpected, left the country in a state of shock, confusion and trepidation. The nation had been robbed of its god-like emperor, the man who had been regarded as China's Marx, Lenin and Stalin, its philosopher, liberator and iron-handed ruler, and who had set the country on a radical new course. Mao had been both loved and feared and, while not enjoying unfettered power, had been the dominant and most charismatic influence on the Chinese polity during the previous 27 years, able to force his opinions upon his colleagues, as the 'Great Leap' and 'Cultural Revolution' experiments demonstrated. With the death of its 'Great Helmsman' the nation lost an important unifying force, and a violent inter-dynasty succession struggle appeared likely.

The two rivals for Mao's mantle were Jiang Qing, supported by her 'Gang of Four', and Deng Xiaoping. Deng, although temporarily in hiding, enjoyed the support of the majority of the state bureaucracy, the regional PLA commanders, many of whom had been trained by Zhou Enlai during his period as deputy director of Huangpu Military Academy, and of many old former 'Long March' party colleagues, including Li Xiannian (the one-time Oyuwan soviet leader) and Marshal Ye Jianying (a former Paris 'work study' intellectual). The 'Gang of Four', by contrast, could only count on the support of radical young students, trade unionists and party activists and of the recently reformed urban militias.

Recognising this, Jiang Qing acted with alacrity and attempted to persuade Hua Guofeng, 1st Vice-Chairman of the CPC, to support her claim to the party chairmanship at an emergency Politbureau meeting which was convened within hours of Mao's funeral. Hua, however, refused to side with Jiang and was himself elected chairman of the CPC and MAC. On 7 October, facing mounting disorder at the provincial level and under pressure from PLA generals, Hua ordered the arrest of the 'Gang of Four', who were contriving to stage militia coups in Shanghai and Peking. This decision proved to be popular and was greeted by large rallies critical of the autocratic Jiang Qing and supportive of Hua Guofeng in all China's major cities, including Shanghai, during October 1976.

The Hua Interregnum: 1977-1978

Hua Guofeng, the new head of the CPC, appeared to be in an unusually powerful position in November 1976 combining, in an unprecedented fashion, the three posts of the party chairmanship, MAC chairmanship and state premiership. In reality, however, Hua's position was precarious and he proved to be only a compromise stop-gap leader.

Hua's rise to the top at the age of only 56 was meteoric by the standards of Communist China. He was born near Tiayuan in Shanxi province in northern China in May 1920, the illegitimate son of a rich landlord's daughter who, after being disowned by her family, later married a communist underground labour organiser. Despite this troubled background, however, Hua enjoyed a relatively high standard of education, studying up to secondary level. He was too young to have taken part in the 'Long March', but joined the Communist Party in 1938 and served as a propagandist and political commissar during the 'Liberation War' and Civil War of 1938-49. Following the Communist Revolution of 1949, Hua was posted to Mao Zedong's home province of Hunan. Here he began a steady climb up the party ladder, serving first as a county party committee secretary before eventually rising to become provincial party chief in December 1970.

During his years in Hunan, Hua gained the reputation of being a skilled economist and agronomist, with particular expertise in the fields of irrigation and land reform, and also as an efficient party organiser and intelligence worker. He proved adept at adapting to the frequent changes in the central party line, passing with ease through the disruption of the 'Cultural Revolution' by displaying a useful mixture of Maoist idealism and Zhouist pragmatism. Hua was elected a member of the CPC Central Committee in April 1969 and two years later was brought to Peking, at Mao Zedong's request, to work in the State Council in the economic and scientific spheres as an assistant to the ailing Zhou Enlai. He was further promoted in April 1973, becoming a member of the CPC Politbureau, and in January 1975, at the National People's Congress, was appointed the sixth-ranking Vice-Premier in the PRC and the new minister of public security, a key post during a period of top-level political in-fighting. Hua stood on what must be termed the 'centre-left' of the CPC, loyally supporting the policies of Mao Zedong but opposing the excesses of the 'Gang of Four'. This made him an acceptable choice as an interim leader. Hua's claims to the succession were further strengthened by two factors. Firstly, with Deng Xiaoping in hiding and temporary disgrace, a key, moderate party bureaucrat and Deng supporter who controlled the PLA, Marshal Ye Jianying, gave firm support to Hua in the 1976 succession contest. Secondly, and above all, Mao Zedong, impressed by Hua's work in his native Hunan — work which included the construction of a huge, laudatory display hall in Mao's home village of Shaoshan and the famous Shaoshan irrigation project — designated him his new 'chosen successor' during 1975-6, allegedly writing a private note to Hua in April 1976 which concluded with the words, 'with you in charge, my heart is at ease'.[1]

Hua, being relatively unknown and lacking the charisma and popular support enjoyed by Mao Zedong, sought, once having been elected as party chairman, to project himself more widely during 1977, and set about disseminating a minor 'cult of personality'. However, Hua's position as head of government remained uncertain, leading, as he did, a coalition divided between committed Maoists and Zhouist-Dengist modernisers. Hua tried at first to isolate Deng by launching a campaign of criticism in November 1976. This failed, however, to gain support, and instead wall posters began to appear in Peking in December 1976 calling for the restoration to office of Deng Xiaoping. This movement gained the support of leading bureaucrats, ministers, provincial party leaders and military commanders who, fearing popular disorders on the anniversary of the Tienanmen Square incident, agreed to Deng's return to high office at an enlarged Politbureau meeting in March 1977. The decision, which was greeted by enthusiastic processions all over China during April 1977, marked the beginning of a shift in power away from Hua Guofeng and into the hands of Deng Xiaoping.

Deng's restoration to office was confirmed at the third plenum meeting of the CPC's 10th Central Committee in July 1977, which also exonerated him from any blame for the Tienanmen demonstration and announced its decision to expel the 'Gang of Four' from the party. The 'Four Modernisations' policy of Deng and Zhou was also given increased prominence during 1977; Dengist supporters, such as Zhao Cangbi (the new minister of public security), were rehabilitated; radical leaders were ousted as party first secretaries in twelve of the nation's 26 provinces and autonomous regions (including those of Yunnan, Heilongjiang, Liaoning, Gansu, Zhejiang, Guizhou, Anhui and Jiangsu) and replaced by centrist moderates. A number of films and plays which had previously been suppressed were now shown, as the intellectual climate became more open and liberal.

The reconstruction of the Chinese political system along its pre-1965 lines gained impetus in 1977, with the calling of the 11th CPC Congress between August 12 and 18. In his four-hour speech to Congress, Chairman Hua formally announced that the 'Cultural

---

[1] The authenticity and true meaning of this note has, however, been questioned by leading figures in China since Hua's fall from power.

Revolution' had been brought to an end in October 1976 with the overthrow of the 'Gang of Four' and that the CPC leadership would concentrate now on re-establishing true Leninist-Maoist party democracy with a collective form of executive decision-taking and the encouragement of internal debate and criticism. The composition of the 11th Congress was very similar to that of 1956. The PLA's influence was much reduced compared to its 1969 and 1973 level. Many young 'Gang' supporters were excluded, and 40% of the new Central Committee comprised cadres who had been purged between 1966-69.[1] This Central Committee went on to elect a new Politbureau and Standing Committee on 19 August 1977 (see Table 5).

TABLE 5 : The CPC Politbureau and Standing Committee in August 1977

Standing Committee

Hua Guofeng (Chmn)	Deng Xiaoping	Wang Donxiang[2]
Ye Jianying	Li Xiannian[4]	

Politbureau

FULL MEMBERS	Peng Chong[3]	Fang Yi[3]
Xu Xiangqian[4]	Chen Yongkui[2]	Ulanhu[3]
Nie Rongzhen[4]	Ji Dengkui[1]	Wu De[2]
Liu Bocheng[3]	Li Disheng[1]	
Wei Guoqing[3]	Yu Qiuli[3]	ALTERNATE MEMBERS
Su Zhenhua[4]	Ni Zhifu[1]	Zhao Ziyang[3]
Zhang Tingfa[1]	Geng Biao[3]	Chen Muhua[3] (f)
Chen Xilian[2]	Xu Shiyou[3]	Saifudin[2]

(f) — female

NOTES [1] Supporters of Hua Guofeng. [2] Firm Maoists. (Wang Donxiang had been Mao's personal bodyguard and was the man who arrested the 'Gang of Four' in October 1976). [3] Supporters of Deng Xiaoping. [4] Supporters of Ye Jianying but allied to Deng Xiaoping.

---

[1] The new Central Committee comprised 201 full members, 71 (35%) of whom had not been members of the previous 10th Central Committee and 20 of whom had been promoted from alternate membership. It also comprised 132 alternate members, 75 (57%) of whom were new faces. The 29 first secretaries of provincial, autonomous municipality and autonomous region level were all given seats in the new Central Committee and military representation was stabilised at 30%. The average age of the 11th Central Committee was 63.

Following the purge of the 'Gang of Four' and the recent deaths of Mao Zedong, Zhou Enlai, Zhu De (6 July 1976), Kang Sheng (2 April 1975) and Dong Biwu (10 December 1975), the new Politbureau and Standing Committee necessarily included many new faces. In addition, the 11th Congress adopted a new party constitution which tightened up the admission procedure for entry into the party and reintroduced the system of probation for new party entrants. It also established special new 'discipline commissions' at the county level and above, to investigate the work of the CPC's members, particularly the 17 million younger activists (50% of the CPC total) who had joined the party since the 'Cultural Revolution'. The aim was to root out 'renegades' and to deal with what Ye Jianying referred to as the 'serious problem of impurity.'[1]

The changes made in the Politbureau at the 11th CPC Congress, with the induction of ten new full members, gave Deng Xiaoping a clear majority within the party's most important executive body. Deng's authority was further increased with the appointment of his protégé, Hu Yaobang, as Director of the CPC's Organisation Department in charge of party appointments. Hu set about constructing chargesheets against the leftist Maoists, Wang Donxiang, Chen Xilian, Chen Yongkui and Wu De, with a view to their dismissal. He and Deng were supported by a plethora of posters attacking radical Maoism and the 'Gang of Four' which sprang up on what became known as 'Democracy Wall' in Peking.

Deng needed to be cautious in the extent of his criticisms of Mao's past actions, since the former party chairman remained a respected and popular figure. Gradually, however, a policy of 'de-Maoisation' and 'de-mythologisation' was pursued. It became recognised that Mao Zedong had been human and had made mistakes, although the worst excesses of the period between 1966 and 1975 were still blamed on the pernicious influence of Jiang Qing and the 'Gang of Four'. Mao's achievements as the leader of China's liberation war and successful revolution and his work during the initial years of reconstruction were subject to particular praise. Thus a new volume of Mao's selected works covering the pre-'Great Leap' period, 1949-57, was published in April 1977, edited by Hua Guofeng. These early, moderate and pragmatic works were taken as representing 'true Maoism' setting out as they did a sensible and

[1] Eight million of the CPC's 35 million members had joined the party between 1969 and 1973 and seven million between 1973 and 1977. Many of these were ill-educated workers, peasants and soldiers who had been recruited by radical supporters of the 'Gang of Four'.

balanced agenda for economic development in line, in many respects, with the new Hua-Deng modernisation programme.

While Maoism was being reintroduced during 1977-8, the political system was also being reconstructed along more open and democratic lines. Special broad national conferences were called to discuss policy initiatives in specific areas, including defence, science and technology, transport and education, in a 'united front' manner which recalled the period between 1949 and 1954. Popular views were articulated in an unprecedentedly open manner on 'Democracy Wall' during 1977 and 1978, with one young writer, Wei Jingsheng (29), courageously calling for 'the Fifth Modernisation — Democracy'. Finally the Fifth National People's Congress met between 26 February and 5 March 1978 to adopt a new constitution and approve a new economic plan. Concurrent with this Congress a special Chinese People's Political Consultative Conference (CPPCC) was held, presided over by Deng Xiaoping, incorporating intellectuals, former bourgeois groups and overseas Chinese.

The Fifth NPC appointed Ye Jianying as chairman of its Standing Committee, and thus the country's effective Head of State, and Hua Guofeng as Prime Minister, along with 13 vice-premiers.[1] It also adopted a new constitution which strengthened the organs of state power and restored the legal institutions (including the Supreme People's Procuratorate) and civil rights which had been abrogated during the 'Cultural Revolution'. The Fifth NPC also approved a radical Dengist economic programme of modernisation, mechanisation, improved education and more open commerce.

The Rise of Deng and the Eclipse of Hua: 1978 – 1981

By December 1978 Deng Xiaoping had become firmly established as the dominant force in Chinese politics and was presiding over a major restructuring of China's economy and political system and a reappraisal of the country's international role and its relationship with the outside world. Deng nominally still held only the positions of party vice-chairman, state vice-premier, vice-chairman of the MAC and chief-of-staff to the PLA, while Hua Guofeng combined the posts of party chairman, MAC chairman and state premier. Real authority, however, now rested with Deng.

[1] The 13 vice-premiers appointed by the 5th NPC were: Deng Xiaoping, Li Xiannian, Xu Xiangqian, Ji Dengkui, Yu Qiuli, Chen Xilian, Geng Biao, Chen Yongkui, Fang Yi, Wang Zhen, Gu Mu, Kang Shien and Chen Moruo.

This became clear between 18 and 22 December 1978 when, following a special month-long 'working conference'[1], the 3rd Plenum of the 11th CPC Central Committee met. A compromise was agreed upon at this meeting, whereby Chairman Hua and his supporters were allowed to retain their senior posts in return for agreeing to support the implementation of Deng's economic modernisation and rehabilitation programme. The Plenum thus saw the introduction into the Politbureau of four important Deng supporters — Chen Yun, Deng Yingchao, Wang Zhen and Hu Yaobang. Chen Yun (73) was a veteran economic planning expert who had been the architect of the successful early 1950s and 1962-65 'recovery programmes' before being subsequently purged in 1959 and 1966. He was now made a vice-chairman of the CPC, a fifth-ranking member of the Politbureau's Standing Committee and head of the new Central Commission for Inspecting Discipline (CCID). Deng Yingchao (74) was the late Zhou Enlai's widow. Wang Zhen (70) became a vice-premier in charge of the arms industry. Hu Yaobang (63) was soon to be elected the party's General-Secretary. Besides these four, nine additional Dengists were also introduced into the Central Committee. This was rapidly followed by the rehabilitation and rescindment of charges against the late Peng Dehuai and Liu Shaoqi and other less well-known former party officials, bureaucrats and intellectuals.[2]

In addition, the historic 3rd Plenum declared that the two-year campaign against the 'Gang of Four' and its ultra-radical supporters was now officially over and that the party's efforts should in future be concentrated upon 'socialist modernisation' and the enhancement of living standards. This was to be achieved through the launching of a new economic strategy which would combine closer central scrutiny of plans by a new State Economic Commission with decentralisation in their implementation, giving managers wider scope to use their initiative, and through the raising of material incentives. The new programme also looked for a major expansion of the educational sector and an improvement in the level of technical skills.

---

[1] At this meeting the verdict on the April 1976 Tienanmen demonstrations was reversed, the popular movement now being described as 'completely revolutionary'.

[2] Peng Zhen (77), Peking's mayor prior to the 'Cultural Revolution', was reinstated in his old post in February 1979.

The new man behind this radical shift in policy was Deng Xiaoping. Deng, a diminutive (4'10") 74-year-old, was born in prosperous Sichuan province in August 1904. He came from a similar bourgeois, mandarin background to Zhou Enlai and was a fellow member of the CPC in Paris in 1924, before later studying in Moscow in 1926.[1] He had worked under Mao Zedong at the Jiangxi Soviet between 1931-35, becoming a close and early supporter of the man who was later to become party leader. Deng served as a leading political commissar to the PLA during both the 'Long March' in 1934-36 and in the liberation struggle and civil war of 1937-49.[2] Deng's primary skills were, however, as an efficient and intelligent administrator, gaining entry to the Politbureau in 1956 and working as a powerful Secretary-General (1956-63) prior to the 'Cultural Revolution' in tandem with the Head of State, Liu Shaoqi, and Prime Minister, Zhou Enlai.[3] During this period Deng worked closely with Soviet economic advisers and invariably adhered to the Moscow line, supporting Khrushchev in 1956 in his criticisms of Stalin and the 'cult of personality'. Deng opposed the 'Great Leap' communalisation programme and, having fallen out with his former close friend Mao Zedong after 1960, he had been dismissed from his posts during the 'Cultural Revolution', subjected to a humiliating 'street trial', sent with his wife Cho Lin to Nanchang (Jiangxi province) for 're-education through labour' in a tractor factory and threatened with expulsion from the party. He was saved from harsher punishment by his influential patron Zhou Enlai. Deng, however, differed in many ways from the courteous former Premier, being a more direct and abrasive personality and more élitist and 'rightist' in outlook. He believed passionately in the need to modernise China's economy and raise living standards through the formation of expert managerial teams and the encouragement

[1] Deng, whose father was a substantial Hakka landlord and local regiment leader, had enjoyed an education up to secondary level. He was converted to communism during the years he spent working at the Schneider-Creusot arms factory in Paris between 1920-6.

[2] During the 'Long March' Deng had served as a political commissar to Mao's 'First Front Army' and during the liberation struggle and civil war he had acted as chief political commissar to Liu Bocheng's 129th Division (later renamed the Second Field Army) of the CPC's Eighth Route Army.

[3] Deng had earlier been elected to the CPC Central Committee in April 1945; had served as 1st Secretary of the South-western Region of the new PRC between 1949-52; and had worked as a vice-premier, specialising in economic and administrative affairs, between 1952-4.

of workers through material incentives, and he placed a low priority on Marxist theories and ideology. His favourite dictum was 'Practice is the sole criterion for testing truth'.

Deng now, in 1978, at the twilight of his career, sought progress quickly and was willing at first to tolerate a liberalisation in the political and social climate to encourage enterprise and ability to flourish. There was a visible 'thaw' in CPC cultural and political control during 1978/9, which, like the 'Hundred Flowers' departure of 1956/7, rapidly got out of hand, as pent-up popular grievances were ventilated. Radical posters demanding Western-style human rights were posted on 'Democracy Wall' in Peking and new, low-cost and self-published political journals began to be circulated. Rural peasants marched to Peking in January 1979 demanding economic reforms, and students, coming home to Shanghai and Hangzhou (Hangchow) for the Spring Festival, rioted and refused to return to the countryside to continue their 'education' under the old Maoist system. Some of these actions and demonstrations were controlled from above by Dengist supporters utilising and directing 'public opinion' in their power struggle against Hua Guofeng. Others, however, developed a dangerous spontaneity of their own. This persuaded Deng, in February 1979, to sanction a crackdown against the 'democracy movement'. Wall posters were removed, protesters arrested and exemplary sentences were meted out to over-exuberant offenders.[1]

These and subsequent actions established the new limits for dissent. They did not, however, presage a sudden return to Maoist orthodoxy and autocracy.[2] Instead, progress continued to be made towards restoring balance and justice ('socialist legality') to the political system and inserting a limited degree of democracy under the umbrella of party control, returning the Chinese polity to its early Leninist roots and ideals.

These intentions were made clear in June 1979 when the National People's Congress was called to meet for a second session: it was henceforth to meet on a regular annual basis. The NPC adopted a new Dengist economic plan, approved the appointment of three

---

[1] Wei Jingsheng was, for example, sentenced to 15 years' imprisonment in October 1979.

[2] Later, in 1980, Article 45 of the constitution, which gave citizens the right to free speech and to write large character posters, was deleted, as, in 1982, was the right to strike.

new vice-premiers (Chen Yun, Bo Yibo and Yao Yilin), and passed seven new constitutional laws. These enhanced the role of the people's courts and procuratorates, codified legal rights, extended the election of People's Congress delegates to the county level and created a measure of choice by allowing more candidates to stand than the number of places available. In addition, the NPC was told that, contrary to Mao's 1966-76 statements, the need for turbulent class struggle no longer existed in China and that all efforts should be concentrated upon developing its producing forces. This recalled the verdict of the 1956 CPC Congress and, taken in combination with Ye Jianying's review of the 30-year history of Communist China at the 4th Plenum of the 11th Central Committee, could be taken as implicitly criticising the Maoist approach to economic development.

Chairman Hua was unhappy with such direct criticism of post-1957 Maoism, a philosophy with which he himself had been closely associated, and with the clear Dengist shift in policy direction. His anxieties were shared by more radical Maoists and by lower level party workers and bureaucrats who had prospered during the 'Cultural Revolution' and by politically active middle-ranking army officers. This group, known as the 'whateverist' faction as a result of their unswerving support for anything Chairman Mao said, remained a minority in the post-1976 Chinese polity. However, their position was temporarily strengthened during 1979 as a result of the teething troubles connected with Deng's modernisation drive and criticism of Deng's decision to invade Vietnam (see Part Four).

The Maoist revival proved, however, only to be fleeting. In 1980 the 'whateverist' faction was fatally weakened and Deng Xiaoping's grip on power made unassailable as a result of further victories for the Deng faction within the Central Committee and at the National People's Congress.

At the Fourth Plenum of the 11th Central Committee in September 1979, two powerful and once-purged Dengists appointed to the Politbureau, Peng Zhen and Zhao Ziyang. At the Fifth Plenum, in February 1980, the four remaining Maoist 'whateverists', Wang Donxiang, Ji Dengkui, Chen Xilian and Wu De, were finally forced to resign their party and state posts; the late Liu Shaoqi was fully rehabilitated and placed second in China's pantheon of heroes behind Mao; Hu Yaobang and Zhao Ziyang were promoted to the Politbureau's Standing Committee; and the Secretariat was revived as the day-to-day powerhouse of the CPC, with Hu Yaobang as its General-Secretary working with ten other committed Dengist members.[1]

These changes gave Deng Xiaoping a firm hold over the Chinese polity and furthered its return to pre-1966 constitutional norms. Deng was attempting during this period; firstly, to create a new collective form of party leadership which would share the workload and provide continuity after his death; secondly, to effect a greater separation between the party, state and military spheres of government, following their convergence during the 'Cultural Revolution'; thirdly, to provide a series of checks and balances which would prevent the concentration of power in the hands of any single body or person; and lastly, to define more clearly areas of responsibility and establish proper lines of accountability within a political system which would still be dominated from above by the CPC.

The years between 1979-80 thus saw the political role of the army being further reduced, with the PLA being slowly turned into a more specialised and professional body under a new chief-of-staff, General Yang Dezhi (70), who replaced Deng Xiaoping in that position in February 1980. Army funds and manpower numbers were squeezed during this period, as all efforts were concentrated on economic modernisation, with the military lagging behind a poor fourth in the list of the 'Four Modernisations'.

At the workplace level, the all-pervading 'revolutionary committees' and communes, which had been features of the 'Cultural Revolution' era, were dismantled and replaced by a new system of workshop democracy, giving workers' congresses the power to dismiss their managers. Communal 'responsibility systems' were introduced in agriculture, whereby individual households contracted to supply set quotas and were allowed independently to market any surplus. At the county and provincial

---

[1] The Politbureau's Standing Committee (average age 70) comprised after this meeting: Hua Guofeng, Ye Jianying, Deng Xiaoping, Li Xiannian, Chen Yun (Chairman of the State Financial and Economic Commission), Zhao Ziyang and Hu Yaobang. The Secretariat comprised: Hu Yaobang, Wan Li (Chairman of the State Agricultural Commission), Wang Renzhong, Fang Yi (Chairman of the State Scientific and Technology Commission), Gu Mu (Chairman of the State Economic Commission), Song Renqiong, Yu Qiuli (Chairman of the State Energy Commission), Yang Dezhi, Hu Qiaomu (President of the Academy of Social Sciences), Yao Yilin (Chairman of the State Planning Commission) and Peng Chong. Xi Zhongxun (the former party 1st Secretary of Guangdong) was added to the Secretariat in July 1981.

level, the interference of party cadres in state concerns was similarly diminished.

Finally, at the apex of the political system a significant move towards the separation of state and party officeholders took place at the National People's Congress (Third Session) of August-September 1980. Deng Xiaoping, along with Li Xiannian, Chen Yun, Xu Xiangqian and Wang Zhen, all elderly Politbureau members, resigned their positions as State Vice-Premiers and Hua Guofeng stood down as State Premier.[1] Yang Jingren, Zhang Aiping (70) and the foreign minister, Huang Hua (67), became the new Vice-Premiers, while Zhao Ziyang was appointed the new State Premier.

Deng intended Zhao Ziyang to concentrate on overseeing the Chinese economy and state bureaucracy while his other protégé, Hu Yaobang, would concentrate on party work and ideology in a duumvirate which Deng, during the next quinquennium, would supervise and see firmly established in power in preparation for his own eventual retirement from politics. Such a duumvirate would, he hoped, finally solve the succession problem which Mao had failed to address and would ensure that Dengist policies would endure into the next century. It was thus no surprise when, at the Sixth Plenary Session of the 11th Central Committee in June 1981, Hua Guofeng was finally ousted as Party Chairman, replaced by Hu Yaobang, and demoted to the position of last-ranking Party Vice-Chairman.[2]

The Trial of the 'Gang of Four': November 1980 – January 1981

Hua Guofeng's demise became inevitable once the NPC's Standing Committee formally decided in September 1980 to place on trial the 'Gang of Four', Chen Boda and five senior military colleagues of the former PLA leader Lin Biao on charges of treason against the Chinese state. This decision was taken as a means of finally bringing the curtain down on the 'Cultural Revolution' era, while at the same time satisfying an evident popular desire for retribution. It was

[1] Wang Renzhong also resigned as a vice-premier to take up a major party post, while the Maoist Dazhai 'model peasant', Chen Yongkui, was ousted following allegations of corruption. Deng's longtime friend and colleague, Wan Li, became the new 1st Vice-Premier and thus second-in-command to Zhao Ziyang.

[2] Hua's post as chairman of the MAC was taken over by Deng, ending the traditional combination of the post with that of the party chairmanship.

hoped that the trial would be smooth and uncontentious, with the accused humbly confessing to their crimes in return for the grant of lenient sentences. In such a manner, the reputations of Mao Zedong and Hua Guofeng would be protected. These plans were undermined, however, by the actions of the unrepentant Jiang Qing.

The historic trial opened on 20 November 1980 with the 'Gang' members being charged with plotting to overthrow the party and state leadership and of framing and persecuting over 700 000 officials and leaders, 34 800 of whom subsequently died.[1] In addition they were accused of having contrived an armed rebellion in Shanghai in 1976. The Lin Biao clique was charged with attempting to assassinate Mao Zedong in 1971 and plotting to seize power in a *coup d'état*. The trial took place predominantly in private before 35 judges of a Special Court of the Supreme People's Court and was engineered by the authorities. Jiang Qing refused, however, to co-operate with the State prosecution, and asserted that she had all along acted as the obedient wife of Mao Zedong, carrying out the late Chairman's express orders. Jiang stated tersely, 'Whomever he told me to bite, I bit'. These claims were rejected by the chief prosecutor and by the party-controlled press, which declared that while Mao had made mistakes, they were 'entirely different in nature from the crimes of the Gang'. Zhang Chunqiao also protested his innocence and remained defiantly silent. The other eight accused admitted their guilt.

The trial closed on 29 December 1980 and a month later the judges gave their verdicts. Jiang and Zhang were sentenced to death with a two-year reprieve, the other eight accused were sentenced to terms of imprisonment ranging from 16 years to life.[2] These punishments were set at a level harsh enough to satisfy the public's craving for vengeance without creating new martyrs around which the remnant ultra-leftist forces could gather.

---

[1] Western estimates put the true figure of 'Gang'-induced deaths at close to 400 000.

[2] Wang Hongwen was sentenced to life imprisonment; Yao Wenyuan to 20 years; Chen Boda (now aged 76), Huang Yongsheng (former chief-of-general staff) and Jiang Tengjiao (a former Nanjing air force political commissar) to 18 years; Wu Faxian (a former air force commander) and Li Zuopeng (the former 1st political commissar to the navy) to 17 years; and Qiu Huizuo (the former deputy chief-of-staff) to 16 years. The death penalty on Jiang Qing and Zhang Chunqiao was commuted to life imprisonment in March 1983.

This 'show trial' served to end the political careers of the infamous 'Gang of Four'. It also hastened the demise of Hua Guofeng, who was implicated in many of the 'Gang's' later misdeeds during his period as minister of public security. It further reduced the standing of the PLA, five of whose former leaders were arraigned before the court. The primary purpose of the trial was, however, to bring to a close an unfortunate chapter in Communist China's history and allow the new administration to make a fresh start, concentrating in a united fashion on its vast modernisation programme. Further trials of lower-level 'Gang' supporters and sympathisers would continue in the years ahead, but emphasis was now to shift towards constructive planning for the future.[1] Thus, six months after the trial, on 29 July 1981, the CPC Central Committee published an authoritative official verdict on Mao Zedong and the last 20 years of his life, the 'Resolution on Certain Questions in the History of Our Party since the Founding of the People's Republic'. In this document, Mao's contribution to the building of the CPC and PLA, to victory in the liberation war and the consequent creation of the People's Republic, and to the safeguarding of the nation's independence, unity and security was recognised and praised. He was, however, criticised for becoming tyrannical and obsessed with a misguided leftist line during the last 20 years of his life, culminating in the disastrous 'Cultural Revolution'. Mao was thus 'de-deified' and slavish worship of his thought and writings was now frowned upon. Instead Mao's was seen to be just one of the many contributions to the creation and development of Chinese communist thinking, in what became a new vogue for eclecticism and collectivism.

The Deng-Hu-Zhao Triumvirate: 1981-1986

By the middle of 1981 Deng Xiaoping had firmly established himself as the controlling force in the Chinese polity. As a former 'close comrade in arms' of Mao Zedong, a veteran of the Jiangxi Soviet and the 'Long March' and as the 'designated heir' of the popular Zhou Enlai, Deng enjoyed the legitimacy which came from seniority in the patriarchal Chinese political system — a legitimacy and authority which the 'upstart' Hua Guofeng had lacked. Secondly, he enjoyed,

---

[1] The verdicts on 300 000 people who were wrongly arrested and persecuted during the 'Cultural Revolution' were reversed during the next two years.

as the Tienanmen Square rallies of 1976 and 1977 had demonstrated, a significant measure of genuine public support and affection. Thirdly, and above all, Deng had built up during his lengthy army, state and party career, a network of personal allies and 'clients' spread throughout the upper reaches of the Chinese administrative machine, which enabled him to put together a dominant new Dengist 'modernising coalition' with a clear majority within the CPC Central Committee and Politbureau. Despite such personal dominance, however, Deng chose not to seek the top offices of power — the posts of party leader and Prime Minister — for himself.[1] Instead, he remained nominally only a party vice-chairman and chairman of the MAC, preferring instead to govern from backstage and to concentrate on establishing and enhancing the authority of his protégés and hoped-for successors, Zhao Ziyang and Hu Yaobang. These two men, both more than ten years younger than the septuagenarian Deng, assumed charge of the day-to-day administration of Chinese affairs, leaving Deng to concentrate upon longer-term strategic planning. The two new governors came from sharply differing backgrounds; both, however, had been close and long-term associates of Deng Xiaoping and both shared his pragmatic political ideals.

Zhao Ziyang (b. 1919), the well-educated son of a wealthy Henan province landlord, joined the Communist Youth League in 1932 and became a full member of the CPC in 1938, working underground as a party official in his home region during the liberation struggle and civil war of 1939-49. He first rose to prominence when implementing the land reform programme in Guangdong province between 1951 and 1962, becoming a close ally of the moderate-minded local party 1st secretary Tao Zhu[2] and emerging as the youngest party 1st secretary in the country when Tao was promoted and brought to Peking in April 1965. Encouraged by the work of Liu Shaoqi and Deng Xiaoping, Zhao, as provincial party general-secretary and director of the rural works department,

[1] Deng was, in fact, offered the post of party chairman at both the November 1980 and June 1981 CPC Central Committee meetings. He declined the offer, however, on the grounds of age, stating his inability to meet the punishing workload necessary and calling on the party to look to the future instead and to appoint the younger Hu Yaobang.

[2] Tao Zhu, who briefly rose to become the fifth most powerful man in the Chinese polity in 1965, when appointed head of the CPC Propaganda Department, was purged at the height of the 'Cultural Revolution' in January 1967 and died of cancer in Hefei prison (Anhui province) in November 1969.

introduced an entrepreneurial reform programme in Guangdong during the early 1960s, but found himself the object of attack during the 'Cultural Revolution'. During this dark period, he was sacked from his post in January 1967, paraded through the streets of Canton in a dunce's cap and sent to a remote May Seventh Cadre School in Nei Monggol (Inner Mongolia) for 're-education'. Zhao, however, enjoyed a measure of protection by Zhou Enlai and was rehabilitated in 1971, being given first a lowly party post in Nei Monggol, then transferred back to Guangdong in 1972, before, in November 1975, being appointed party 1st secretary of Sichuan, China's largest province (population 100 million) and the home of Deng Xiaoping.[1] Here Zhao made his reputation through the introduction of a series of innovative and liberalising economic reforms, which reduced bureaucratic interference, encouraged private agriculture and factory self-management, improved material incentives and allowed free rural markets to operate. These reforms, which were later to be termed the 'Sichuan Experience', proved successful, boosting local grain production by 25% within three years, and caught the attention of Peking and, in particular, Deng Xiaoping.[2] Zhao was thus co-opted into the Politbureau as a candidate member in August 1977 and was sent abroad to accompany Chairman Hua on his tour of Romania during August 1978, before rising meteorically to the position of State Premier and CPC Standing Committee member during the following two years.

The diminutive (5'1") Hu Yaobang lacked the provincial administrative and economic expertise of Zhao Ziyang. He possessed, however, extensive experience of central party organisation and had long been a close confidant of Deng Xiaoping. Born into a poor family of peasant farmers in Hunan province in 1915, Hu left home at the age of 14 to join the communists as a child soldier. He became involved in propaganda and organisational work for the CPC, serving directly under Deng Xiaoping during the

---

[1] Zhao was also elected to the CPC Central Committee for the first time in August 1973.

[2] Zhao's contacts with Deng went as far back as the liberation war period, when they had both worked in the Jin-Ji-Lu-Yu border region. Between 1957-65, when Zhao was serving as CPC secretary-general in Guangdong and Deng as General-Secretary of the central party machine, the contacts between the two men became closer and more frequent. When Deng was disgraced for a second time in 1976 and went into hiding in Guangdong, Zhao came specially from Sichuan to hold secret discussions with him.

'Long March' and the 1937-49 liberation struggle and civil war. Hu became Deng's loyal and trusted right-hand man, following his patron to south-western China between 1949-51 and to Peking in 1952, where he worked as head of the Communist Youth League. In April 1956 Hu gained entry to the CPC Central Committee and during the early 1960s briefly served as 1st Secretary of Shaanxi province, before being sacked at the start of the 'Cultural Revolution' and sent into the countryside to work on a dairy farm. Hu was rehabilitated in 1972, being appointed Vice-Chancellor of the Institute of Sciences, but was disgraced again in 1976 following the fall of Deng, before being reinstated in 1977 in what proved to be the first step towards Hu's rapid rise to leadership of the CPC in June 1981. Hu lacked a formal education and was a more direct and earthy speaker than the suave and sophisticated Zhao Ziyang. He was, however, equally flexible and pragmatic in his policy outlook, enjoying a reputation as one of the most liberal members of the CPC leadership team.

These three like-minded figures, with their complementary skills, formed a formidable triumvirate anxious to transform China's economy and political system. They continued to give top priority to economic modernisation during the years between 1981 and 1986, introducing a number of innovative new reforms (see Part 3). The new triumvirate also, however, introduced a number of significant political reforms, helping to further restore order and balance to the party-state system, and they engaged in a thorough overhaul of the state, party and PLA bureaucracies, rooting out the remaining Maoist dissidents and promoting to leadership positions a new echelon of skilled and efficient technocrat-administrators.

In pursuit of their first aim, new and innovative party and state constitutions were adopted by the CPC's 12th Congress (1-11 September) and by the 5th National People's Congress's Fifth Session (26 November – 10 December) during the autumn of 1982.

The new party constitution abolished the post of party Chairman and Vice-Chairman and made the General-Secretary (Hu Yaobang) head of the CPC, in charge of convening Politbureau and Standing Committee meetings and overseeing the work of the Secretariat. This returned the CPC to the norm in the communist world and further augmented the importance of the Dengist-dominated Secretariat as the body in charge of day-to-day party administration. A new top-tier party organ was also created at the 12th CPC Congress: the gerontocratic, Central Advisory Commission (CAC), with Deng Xiaoping as its chairman and with membership limited to those with at least 40 years' standing in the CPC.[1] Deng sought to make the CAC a largely powerless retirement centre for senior Politbureau, Standing Committee and Central Committee members, who he hoped would step aside to enable younger men to enter the Politbureau. His success in persuading senior colleagues to step down was, however, limited at the 12th Congress. The membership of the CPC Standing Committee remained largely static, with the powerful, and sometimes critical, figures of Ye Jianying and Li Xiannian retaining their seats and only Hua Guofeng being ousted.[2] Changes were more extensive at the Politbureau, Secretariat (see Table 6) and Central Committee levels. Seven experienced new men, all close allies of Deng Xiaoping, were brought into the Politbureau and four into the Secretariat, while 211 (60%) of the Central Committee's 348 members and alternate members were newcomers, two-thirds of them being under the age of 60.

The new state constitution adopted by the NPC in December 1982 introduced four significant reforms. Firstly, the figurehead posts of State President and Vice-President, which had been abolished in 1975, were now restored. Secondly, people's congresses and committees were re-established below the county level (i.e. in small towns and villages) to take over the political and ideological work which had previously been carried out by commune management committees. Thirdly, the legislative powers of the NPC's Standing Committee were significantly increased and now included the authority to annul the unconstitutional actions of ministers. Fourthly, a new State Central Military Commission (SCMC) was established to oversee the day-to-day activities of the PLA and a new Ministry of State Security was created to take over the internal security duties of the army.

The new 6th National People's Congress met six months later between 6-21 June 1983 and elected Li Xiannian as China's first President since the late Liu Shaoqi in 1969. Zhao Ziyang was elected State Premier, the Mongol, General Ulanhu, became Vice-President, the Peking mayor, Peng Zhen, was chairman of the

---

[1] The new party constitution reserved the chairmen of the MAC, Advisory and Discipline Commissions each a seat on the Politbureau Standing Committee.

[2] Hua Guofeng was re-elected, however to the Central Committee.

TABLE 6 : The CPC Politbureau, Standing Committee, Secretariat and MAC in September 1982[1]

Standing Committee

Hu Yaobang (67)	Ye Jianying (85)	Deng Xiaoping (78)
Zhao Ziyang (63)	Li Xiannian (78)	Chen Yun (77)

Remainder of Politbureau

RE-ELECTED MEMBERS	Peng Zhen	Liao Chengzi
Marshal Xu Xiangqian	Ni Zhifu	Xi Zhongxun
Marshal Nie Rongzhen	Yu Qiuli	Hu Qiaomu
Gen. Zhang Tingfa	Fang Yi	Wan Li
Gen. Wei Guoqing		
Gen. Li Disheng	NEW MEMBERS	ALTERNATE MEMBERS
Gen. Ulanhu	Gen. Yang Dezhi	Chen Muhua (f)
Deng Yingchao (f)	Song Renqiong	Gen. Qin Jiwei
Wang Zhen	Yang Shangkun	Yao Yilin

Secretariat

FULL MEMBERS	Yao Yilin (67)	Gu Mu (68)
Hu Yaobang (Secr-Gen)	Yang Yong (70)	
Xi Zhongxun (69)	Yu Qiuli (70)	ALTERNATE MEMBERS
Chen Pixian (66)	Hu Qili (53)	Hao Jianxui (47) (f)
Deng Liqun (67)	Wan Li (66)	Qiao Shi (57)

Military Affairs Commission

Deng Xiaoping (Chmn)	Ye Jianying	Nie Rongzhen
Yang Shangkun (V-Chmn)	Xu Xiangqian	

Central Advisory Commission

Deng Xiaoping (Chmn)	Xu Shiyou (V-C)	Li Weihan (V-C)
Bo Yibo (V-C)	Tan Zhenlin (V-C)	

Central Commission for Inspecting Discipline

1st Secretary:	2nd Secretary:	Perm. Secretary:
Chen Yun	Huang Kecheng	Wang Heshou

(f) — female

---

[1] Wang Renzhong, Song Renqiong, Fang Yi, Gen. Yang Dezhi, Hu Qiaomu and Peng Chong were removed from the Secretariat during the September 1982 reshuffle. Hua Guofeng, Peng Chong and Chen Yongkui were removed from the Politbureau. Marshal Liu Bocheng retired and Admiral Su Zhen had died. Geng Biao and Gen. Xu Shiyou joined the CAC, as did Gen. Chen Xilian and Wu De, who had been removed from the Politbureau in February 1980.

NPC Standing Committee, and Deng Xiaoping chairman of the new SCMC.[1]

In addition to constitutional reform, the years after 1981 also saw a major streamlining of the state and party bureaucracies and their infusion with new and better educated cadres.

The pruning of the state bureaucracy began soon after Premier Zhao Ziyang's speech in December 1981 in which he fiercely criticised the waste and inefficiency which resulted from the 'overlapping and overstaffed administrations with their multi-tiered departments, crammed full of superfluous personnel and deputy and nominal chiefs who engage in endless haggling and shifts of responsibility'. In 1982 the number of Vice-Premiers was reduced from 13 to 2 and the number of ministries, commissions and agencies under the State Council almost halved from 98 to 52, with staff numbers being slashed by almost a third from a figure of 49 000 to one of 32 000. In addition, the lifetime tenure of officeholders was ended, with a compulsory retirement age limit of 65 years now being imposed for state ministers and many others being encouraged to retire early with 'perks' and a favourable pension. At the lower levels of the state bureaucracy, major efforts were made to weed out the corrupt and obstructive, while a sixth of the country's 20 million officials were temporarily rotated away from their jobs for rectification, reform and retraining.

A similar streamlining and shake-up of party organisation took place after 1983, with a major three-year rectification campaign being launched. During this campaign the credentials and career records of all the CPC's 40 million members were reviewed, with an eye to the removal of obstructive ultra-leftists who had entered the party during the 'Cultural Revolution', as well as those found guilty of corruption. It was hoped to attract into the party, in their stead, a young new generation of personnel imbued with the high technical and educational skills which would be needed for the overseeing and implementation of the Dengist modernisation programme, as Peking began to progressively delegate more responsibilities to the provinces and counties.

---

[1] In 1982 the two Dengist vice-premiers were Wan Li (concentrating on political and legal affairs) and Yao Yilin (concentrating on the economy) and the State Councillors were Yu Qiuli, Geng Biao, Fang Yi, Gu Mu, Kang Shien, Chen Muhua (China's most senior female leader), Bo Yibo, Ji Pengfei, Huang Hua and Zhang Jingfu.

The campaign was directed by Hu Yaobang and overseen by Song Renqiong, head of the Central Committee's organisation department[1], Wang Zhen, president of the central party school, and by Qiao Shi, the party's personnel chief. It met with early success, with the replacement of nine of the 29 provincial, autonomous region and autonomous municipality 1st Party Secretaries (lowering their average age in the process from 63 to 56). By the end of 1984 over 40 000 had been deprived of their party cards. The campaign gained fresh impetus after 1984 when it was decided that officials over the age of 60 should retire and that party committees should in future only oversee the appointment of officials at the immediate level below and not, as before, at levels several rungs down the party ladder. These measures brought significant upward mobility for college-educated CPC members, whose percentage among the party leadership rose from 10% to 40%. Further, in combination with a slow shift to more democratic and secret balloting systems for leadership posts, they served to break up old patronage networks.[2] By 1986 the campaign had succeeded in forcing 900 000 elderly party officials to step down and had resulted in the promotion of 200 000 young and well-educated members to posts at county level and above, as the criterion for cadre promotion now became that of merit rather than seniority.[3]

These reforms of the party and State bureaucracies stirred up, however, fierce opposition among the more traditionalist elements of the CPC élite. In the leftist-controlled provinces of Yunnan, Shanxi and Hunan (the home base for Mao and Hua) the local party leadership proved to be particularly obstructive and the 1983-6 CPC

[1] Song Renqiong was a particularly close friend and colleague of Deng Xiaoping, having served under Deng (and Hu Yaobang) as deputy director of the political department of the 129th Division and the Second Field Army during the liberation struggle and civil war. During the 1950s he had worked as Deputy Secretary-General to the Central CPC and between 1961-6 had headed the party apparatus in North-east China, before being purged during the 'Cultural Revolution'.

[2] Shaanxi province pioneered the switch to more open party electoral systems when, in November 1984, the new provincial 1st Party Secretary was chosen from a list of 13 and elected by a secret ballot of 300 county and provincial party officials. The CPC Central Committee retained, however, the power of veto during this election. In Jiangxi, the first ever female provincial 1st Party Secretary, Wan Shaofen (53), was also appointed during this period.

[3] 4.8 million new members joined the CPC between 1979 and 1984. However, by 1984 still only 4% of party members had enjoyed higher education and only 3.3% were under the age of 25.

'rectification campaign' was turned against 'rightist' members, who were depicted as having, once more, taken the 'capitalist road'. More conservative party traditionalists were equally concerned with the adverse side-effects of Deng Xiaoping's economic liberalisation reforms for rural and, after October 1984, urban areas (see Part 3). Income differentials were widening, unemployment was rapidly rising and material expectations were being fuelled to an excessive and unrealistic degree. In urban centres, China's youth, a generation scarred by the disruptions and persecutions of the previous decade, was becoming increasingly materialistic and rebellious. They began to adopt Western fashions, purchase motorbikes, hi-fis and televisions, and became disorderly at university campuses. They protested over price rises, cadre privileges and the growing level of imports from Japan, and rioted following China's defeat in a soccer match versus Hong Kong in May 1985. These and other developments suggested that Chinese society was becoming increasingly corrupted and amoral, importing many of the evils traditionally associated with the capitalist West. For example, vice rings began to develop in the cities of the eastern seaboard, the murder and crime rates rose sharply between 1982-85 and a new category of 'economic crime' emerged. This involved party and state personnel who became involved in vast black-marketeering, fraud and embezzlement rings as they began to use their positions of authority and their ability to grant or withhold licences to line their own pockets and to keep ahead of artisan and peasant farming neighbours in China's great new economic race.[1]

Faced with such developments, many older party members began during 1985 to argue that Deng's reform experiment had gone too far. It had diminished the role played by, and the prestige once enjoyed by, CPC cadres (ganbu) and had seriously destabilised Chinese society. The most vociferous opposition group were the remnant Maoist traditionalists who began to mount a new campaign calling for a full reversal of the post-1978

---

[1]   By December 1985 a government investigation had found that more than 67 000 party and government officials had been involved in illegal businesses and corrupt practices. The most spectacular included a £53 million smuggling operation in Fujian province and a $1.5 billion import-export embezzlement racket set up by party officials in the free-trade zone of Hainan Island between January 1984 and May 1985.

reforms and a return to the egalitarian commune ideal, with politics firmly 'back in command'. This faction had, however, been reduced to a minority within the upper echelons of the CPC and proved to be largely ineffective. More powerful, influential and extensive was a body of 'pragmatic modernisers' gathered around the veteran Standing Committee member and CCID chief, Chen Yun. This grouping had supported many of Deng's early reforms but felt that now, with social as well as fiscal problems mounting, the pace of change should be slowed and, what they saw as, the dangerous policy of decentralisation and devolution halted. They were anxious to retain firm and centralised party control over China's economy and society and to give increased priority to ideology.

A second source of rising opposition to the Deng reforms was the military, which, with twelve men in the Politbureau in 1982, still retained significant influence. Many senior PLA commanders shared Deng's concern to modernise and professionalise an army whose inadequacies had been made plain during the brief invasion of Vietnam in February-March 1979. They did not like, however, the low priority which had been accorded to the military sector in the 1978-86 development plans (the PLA's share of the state budget falling from 15% in 1978 to only 9% in 1986) and felt that the diminution in the PLA's political role was being carried out too rapidly and that discipline had been allowed to slacken to a dangerous degree. Middle-ranking officers and political commissars who had risen to prominence during the 'Cultural Revolution' and who had been deeply influenced by leftist Maoism were especially antagonistic to the Deng reforms, which, through giving priority to technical ability rather than ideological commitment (expertise rather than 'redness'), appeared to threaten their own promotion prospects.

Deng Xiaoping sought to assuage his internal party critics during the years between 1983 and 1986 through the adoption of a vigorous disciplinarian line against crime. The 'carrot and stick' approach was employed in the drive against official corruption. Salary levels were raised, extravagant 'perks' banned, the scrutiny of spending made more rigorous and punishments made harsher. Resort to the death penalty increased during these years, with more than 10 000 being executed for criminal and economic offences between August 1983 and December 1985. However, most of those punished were drawn either from outside or from the lower and middle rungs of the State and party bureaucracies. The Deng administration proved less willing to take firm action against top level offenders for fear of antagonising an élite which had grown accustomed to its *te-quan* special privileges and reliance on the *guanxi* old-boy network.[1]

Secondly, Deng sought to infuse the CPC with his own brand of socialist ideology and to eradicate destabilising 'ultra-rightist' and Western influences. A collection of his post-1975 speeches and interviews was thus published in 1983 and rapidly sold over 40 million copies. In these *Selected Works*, Deng continued to stress the vital need for economic modernisation to raise living standards, but he also warned against the dangers of greed, selfishness and a reversion to capitalist practices. He called instead for the practical implementation of Marxism in a co-operative spirit to build a successful 'socialism with Chinese characteristics'. In addition, rectification campaigns were launched in 1983 and 1984 directed against the 'spiritual pollution' of decadent bourgeois ideologies and Western materialistic culture, and periodic clampdowns were applied, suppressing the work of 'bourgeois liberal' artists and activists. The Central Committee secretary and party propaganda chief, Deng Liqun, an advocate of Marxist orthodoxy, played a prominent role in these campaigns.

Deng tackled his army opponents head-on during the years between 1983 and 1986. He fought, as chairman of the MAC and SCMC, a series of bruising battles and slowly began to transform the PLA into a modern, slimmed-down, efficient and flexible fighting machine and to oust antagonistic commanders. During these years, the PLA's central bureaucracy was drastically reduced in size by a quarter, with 50 000 senior officers being pensioned off, one million troops disbanded and the number of military regions reduced from eleven to seven.[2] However, to compensate the generals, spending

[1] Particularly notorious in this respect were the families of the veteran Politbureau members Marshal Ye Jianying and Peng Zhen, whose daughter was under suspicion for 'economic crimes'. However, even Deng Xiaoping and Prime Minister Zhao Ziyang have been known to have used their influence to advance the careers of their children and close relatives, arranging scholarships abroad and supporting their rapid promotion to high academic and State administration posts. Such favouritism towards family or clan members formed an essential part of the Chinese mandarin tradition.

[2] The decision to reduce PLA manpower from 4.2 million to 3 million was taken in July 1985 and was expected to be achieved by 1988. Troops were, in addition, to be recruited in future by compulsory conscription and military ranks (which had been abolished in 1965) were restored in 1987. The size of the People's Militia was reduced even more drastically from a figure of 12-15 million to one of barely three million. Demobilisation was handled, however, in a sensitive manner, with major retraining centres being established to equip soldiers for civilian jobs, army factories being converted to light industry establishments and combat veterans being given special preference in employment selection.

per capita on the armed forces was raised, with salary levels being improved, training facilities increased and new weapon systems purchased. This improved the quality, efficiency and morale of the troops remaining.

These palliative initiatives were buttressed by a series of important state, military and party personnel changes which were effected by the Deng-Hu-Zhao triumvirate during 1985. In June and September, thirteen university-trained technocrats (with an average age of 55) were brought into the State Council to take over important security- and economic-related posts and, in July, four new regional military commanders were appointed when eight were retired.[1] The latter move formed part of the PLA's reorganisation programme, with a new clutch of military academy graduates being promoted to leadership posts. The most sweeping changes, however, took place during September 1985 and occurred within the party hierarchy.

Deng Xiaoping recognised that, with his protégés Hu and Zhao now in their late sixties, he needed to bring forward a new 'third echelon' generation of party leaders in their forties and fifties to ensure that his reform programme was continued into the next century. He thus organised, with Hu Yaobang, a dramatic shake-up of the Central Committee and Politbureau in September 1985, the most sweeping since the 'Cultural Revolution'.

At the CPC Central Committee meeting on 16 September more than 130 party veterans were persuaded to retire: 64 from the Central Committee, 37 from the CAC, 30 from the CCID and 10 from the Politbureau. This represented more than a quarter of the party leadership élite and included the ailing, but obstinate, Marshal Ye Jianying (88), the military scientist, Marshal Nie Rongzhen (86), the former leftist commander of Shenyang (Manchuria), Li Disheng (69), the former head of the Air Force, Zhang Tingfa (72), the PLA veterans, Marshal Xu Xiangqian (83) and General Wei Guoqing (67),

---

[1] The three regions of Peking (former commander (FC) General Qin Jiwei), Canton (FC, You Taizhong) and Shenyang (FC, General Li Disheng) remained unchanged in size, but Shenyang now received a new commander, Liu Jingsong. China's other eight military regions were paired into four commands: Lanzhou (FC, Zheng Weishen) and Urumqi (FC, Major-General Xiao Quanfu) into the 'Western Region' commanded by Zhao Xianshu; Chengdu (FC, General Wang Chenghan) and Kunming (FC, Major-General Zhang Zhixiu) into the 'South-Western Region' commanded by Fu Quanyou; Fuzhou (FC, Major-General Jiang Yonghui) and Nanking (FC, General Xiang Shouzi) into the 'Eastern Region' commanded by Xiang Shouzi; and Jinan (FC, Vice-Admiral Rao Shoukun) and Wuhan (FC, General Zhou Shizhang) into the 'Central Region' commanded by Li Jiulong.

the Vice-President, General Ulanhu (79), the party organisers, Song Renqiong (76) and Wang Zhen (77), the veteran Maoist, Wang Donxiang (69), the former foreign minister, Huang Hua (72), defence minister, General Zhang Aiping (75), and Zhou Enlai's widow, Deng Yingchao (81). They retired with honour, a number joining the CAC, and were allowed to retain the use of an official car and comfortable accommodation, and were given pensions and preferential access to medical attention and luxury items.[1] Their departure contrasted starkly with the Maoist purges of the 1960s and served to establish a precedent for honourable and genuine retirement in the gerontocratic Chinese political system.

A day later, a 933-member Special Party National Delegate Conference began a week-long period of deliberations, during which it discussed the new 1986-90 7th Five Year Plan and the proposed personnel promotions. This was only the second time such a Special Conference had been called, the previous occasion being 40 years ago during the liberation war, thus outlining the significance of the changes being contemplated.[2] A third of the conference was made up of 'young' provincial leaders who had been promoted since 1983 and who were sympathetic to the Dengist strategy. Many other delegates were, however, more cautious in their support for Deng's reform experiment. They sided with Chen Yun and would only agree to support Deng's third echelon promotions if Deng agreed, in return, to rein back his economic reform programme and to pay greater attention to ideology and party discipline.

Such a compromise was agreed upon and the Special Conference was concluded with the election of 29 new full members to the CPC Central Committee, 35 new 'alternate' members and the promotion of 27 existing 'alternates'. Three-quarters of these new entrants had a 'college background' and their average age was 50.[3] A week later, on 25 September 1985, the changed Central Committee elected in turn a new Politbureau

[1] Four veterans, including General Li Disheng and Zhang Tingfa, joined the CAC.

[2] A smaller-scale Central Work Conference was also called in September 1965 at the start of the 'Cultural Revolution'. Such delegate conferences were important in legitimising personnel changes in the Central Committee which, according to the strict letter of the CPC's Constitution, should really have awaited the calling of the next Party Congress.

[3] The Special Conference also elected 56 new members to the CAC and 31 to the CCID.

and Secretariat, bringing in six new full Politbureau members, three new members to the Secretariat and promoting two existing 'alternates' in the latter body. (See Table 7).

TABLE 7 : The CPC Politbureau and Secretariat in September 1985

Standing Committee

Hu Yaobang (70)	Deng Xiaoping (81)	Chen Yun (80)
Zhao Ziyang (66)	Li Xiannian (81)	

Remainder of Politbureau

RE-ELECTED MEMBERS	Yu Qiuli	Qiao Shi
Gen. Yang Shangkun	Fang Yi	Hu Qili
Gen. Yang Dezhi		Li Peng
Xi Zhongxun	NEW MEMBERS	
Hu Qiaomu	Wu Xueqian	ALTERNATE Members
Peng Zhen	Tian Jiyun	Gen. Qin Jiwei
Ni Zhifu	Yao Yilin	Chen Muhua (f)

Secretariat

RE-ELECTED MEMBERS	Yu Qiuli (73)	NEW MEMBERS
Hu Yaobang (70)	Hu Qili (56)	Wang Zhaoguo (43)
Chen Pixian (69)	Wan Li (69)	Hao Jianxui (50) (f)
Deng Liqun (70)		Tian Jiyun (56)
Yang Yong (73)		Qiao Shi (61)
		Li Peng (57)

(f) — female

These changes served to reduce still further the political influence of the PLA, which lost nine members from the Politbureau, leaving it with only three full representatives, all of whom were supportive of the Deng modernisation programme: General Yang Dezhi (chief-of-general-staff), General Yang Shangkun (vice-chairman of SCMC), and Yu Qiuli (director of the army's general political department). The changes also considerably strengthened the grip of the Deng-Hu-Zhao triumvirate over the party machine. A third echelon of senior leaders was now in place, and was already almost in full control of the State Council and state ministries and was poised to take over the reins of the CPC. The most prominent members of this echelon were: Hu Qili (56), an English-speaking, Shaanxi-born, engineering graduate and former president of the All China Youth League and mayor of Tianjin (Tientsin), who stood on the liberal reformist wing of the party; Li Peng (57), the adopted son of Zhou Enlai and a Moscow-trained hydroelectric engineer, who was now head of the State Education Commission and a Deputy Premier, taking a special interest in nuclear energy and the heavy industries and frequently acting as China's chief negotiator with the Soviet Union; Tian Jiyun (56), the protégé of Zhao Ziyang (under whom he had served in Sichuan during the mid 1970s) who, as Deputy-Premier, had been the architect of China's recent price reforms; Qiao Shi (61), another Deputy Premier and the new head of the CPC's Organisation Department, who stood on the conservative reformist wing of the CPC and exerted day-to-day control over the party's security apparatus; Wang Zhaoguo (43), a former provincial car factory manager who, having impressed Deng Xiaoping during a provincial tour, had been brought to Peking to work in the CPC Secretariat; and, finally, Li Ruihuan (51), a former carpenter who had been in charge of constructing the mausoleum for Mao Zedong in 1976 and who, although not a member of the Politbureau or Secretariat, had earned considerable praise since 1982 for his innovative work as mayor of China's fourth largest city, Tientsin. These technocrats were being groomed to take over power from the Deng-Hu-Zhao triumvirate, while meanwhile at the provincial and county levels fourth and fifth echelon party cadres in their thirties and forties were similarly being created.[1]

Dengism Endangered? The Reaction Against Reform: 1986-1987

The price paid for the personnel changes of September 1985 was an agreement on the part of Dengist reformers to slow down the pace of economic change during 1986 and to oppose more firmly 'ideological impurity'. This agreement was reached following an

[1] The most prominent member of the up-and-coming 'fourth cadre' was Li Changchun, mayor of the industrial city of Shenyang, who, having introduced a series of bold economic experiments, was promoted in March 1987 to the post of party 1st Secretary of Liaoning province, thus becoming, at the age of 43, the nation's youngest provincial governor.

uncompromising speech at the September 1986 Special Conference by the leader of the conservative wing of the ruling élite, Chen Yun. He castigated the recent adoption of a bourgeois, decadent ideology of 'putting money above all else' and the state and party's abandonment of traditional centralised economic control for a new system of indirectly guiding production through the manipulation of fiscal indicators. Chen's sentiments had been shared by many party colleagues who were concerned with many of the adverse consequences of the recent Dengist decentralising and liberalising economic reforms which had become evident in 1985, a year which had proved to be the most unsettling experienced by China for more than a decade. In the rural sector, 1985 had seen the first sharp fall in grain production for a quinquennium as peasant farmers, now in control of their own acreage, had switched land away from poorly-paying grain towards more lucrative commercial crops. In the urban-industrial sector, the new system of enterprise management and price deregulation had resulted in a sudden and unco-ordinated surge in production, (industrial output increasing at an annual rate of 24% during the first half of 1985 against a target of 8%). Serious and wasteful bottlenecks and a sharp rise in the level of unemployment also occurred. In addition, the year had seen inflation reach an annual level of 22%, the state budget and foreign trade balances moving into serious deficit and regional and social income differentials continuing to widen.

Faced with such problems and criticisms, the reformist wing of the CPC leadership was forced into temporary retreat during the autumn of 1985 and spring of 1986. It agreed to shelve the introduction of further liberalising economic reforms during 1986, which was now designated as a 'year of consolidation', and to raise interest and taxation rates and devalue the currency in an effort to discourage capital investment and foreign imports and thus cool off what was becoming a dangerously overheated economy. In addition, the party and state leadership announced that special credit, fertiliser and price incentives would be introduced to encourage increased grain production. These policy changes succeeded in sharply bringing down the annual rate of economic growth to below 5% during the first half of 1986 and giving a boost to grain sowing. They were buttressed in the ideological sphere by the launch of a major new party rectification campaign in November 1985, under the supervision of the CPC Secretaries Qiao Shi and Wang Zhaoguo, directed against corruption at both local and senior party levels and by the introduction of new regulations in

February 1986 which prohibited party and state officials from engaging in business activities.

During the summer of 1986, however, the reform wing of the party élite[1] regained the ascendancy and began to press for an intensification of the economic reform and liberalisation process. They argued that many of the teething problems associated with the economic reform programme thus far had resulted from the incomplete nature of the changes effected. They believed that further price deregulation was necessary to enable resources to be more efficiently allocated, as was a fuller separation of the party and state machines if factory managers were to be freed from bureaucratic interference. In addition, the more radical members of the Dengist reform faction began to argue that economic restructuring alone would not be sufficient and that a measure of political reform and 'socialist democratisation' was required to achieve an underpinning of popular support and enthusiasm for the new economic system.

In June 1986, on the thirtieth anniversary of the 'Hundred Flowers' movement of 1956/7, a major new liberalising thaw in the cultural sphere was instigated. The thaw was heralded by the appointment as the new minister of culture of Wang Meng (51), an anti-establishment writer who had been subjected to internal exile as a dissident between 1957-79. Wang, working with the CPC's liberal-minded Propaganda Chief Zhu Houze (55)[2], sanctioned a series of radical new plays and novels and began to encourage, in the columns of the party-controlled *People's Daily* and *Red Flag*, the opening of a wide-ranging debate on political reform, with articles calling for a Western-style separation of judicial, legislative and executive powers and for the upgrading and expansion of China's legal system. These literati and academic exchanges formed part of a broader debate which was taking place within élite circles over the nature and extent of the political reforms that would be introduced at the forthcoming CPC Congress in September 1987.

In the midst of this new cultural thaw, the 12th CPC Central Committee met for its 6th Plenum on 28 September 1986 and

[1] The most prominent members of the dominant 'reform faction' were Hu Yaobang, Zhao Ziyang, Hu Qili, Tian Jiyun, Wan Li and Li Ruihuan.

[2] Zhu Houze had replaced the more orthodox Deng Liqun as CPC Propaganda Secretary in June 1985. Zhu, a former 1st Party Secretary of Guizhou province and President of the Communist Youth League, was a close ally of Hu Yaobang and Hu Qili.

approved a new 10 000-character resolution 'designed to clarify certain questions and to formulate the guiding principles for building a socialist society with an advanced culture and ideology'. The resolution, whose aim was to establish a new Dengist ideological orthodoxy, repudiated the Maoist emphasis on class struggle and egalitarianism (equal pay for unequal work) and committed the CPC instead to the continued reform of political and economic structures to build a 'socialism with Chinese characteristics' in which would be applied the principle 'from each according to his ability, to each according to his needs'. In addition, the new ideological charter called for the development of a 'socialist humanism' rejecting the 'pursuit of personal interests at the expense of others', and concerned with 'helping people become better educated and more self-disciplined' and which was rooted firmly in the rule of law.

The Central Committee plenum with its call for the party to concentrate less upon material civilisation (*wuzhi wenming*) and more upon spiritual civilisation (*jingshen wenming*) represented, in many respects, a compromise between the conservative and liberal wings of the reformist élite. Soon after the plenum's ending, however, party liberals were on the offensive again, encouraging an escalation of the campaign for 'political reform'. This campaign was, however, to seriously backfire and lead to a powerful conservative backlash.

The post-June cultural liberalisation campaign had encouraged an intellectual ferment on China's university campuses, with academics playing a leading role in the new debate over future political reform. A prominent figure in this debate was Professor Fang Lizhi, a distinguished astrophysicist and vice-president of the Hefei Institute of Science and Technology in Anhui province. Although a member of the CPC he was a sharp critic of Marxism-Leninism and an advocate of increased democratisation and Westernisation. On 5 December 1986 Professor Fang, with the support of a number of top-level party officials, encouraged his university's students to begin a campaign centred around the specific demand for genuine elections to the local provincial people's assembly. The campaign, however, failed to end when the local authorities agreed to this demand. Instead, the movement acquired a momentum of its own, leading to general student calls for true Western-style democracy, political pluralism and human rights. The new 'Democracy Movement', which recalled that of 1978/9, spread to other provincial universities, including Wuhan,

Kunming, Nanking, Suzhou, Canton, Changsha and Tientsin, during the second and third weeks of December and to Shanghai on 19 December, where it resulted in large and sometimes violent street demonstrations involving crowds of up to 50 000. The government, through the agencies of the police and press, initially treated the demonstrations in a calm and tolerant manner. However, when the protest movement spread to universities in the national capital, Peking, on 23 December, concern mounted and a tougher approach was adopted. On 26 December a ban on protest marches and rallies was imposed in Peking and other major cities and critical editorials warning of retribution for offenders began to appear in the *People's Daily*. However, despite such admonitions, the students of Peking's Qinghua and Beida universities flouted the ban and staged major demonstrations in Tienanmen Square on 1 and 2 January 1987, chanting 'long live democracy' and ostentatiously burning copies of the *People's Daily*. The demonstrations slowly petered out during the second week of January as the students returned home for the Chinese New Year holiday and began to revise for forthcoming examinations. The events of December 1986 and January 1987 were, however, to have serious and continuing repercussions for the liberal wing of the CPC élite.

The CPC's General-Secretary, Hu Yaobang, disappeared from public view on 29 December, being replaced by senior colleagues in meetings scheduled with foreign dignitaries. He had enjoyed close personal links with propaganda chief Zhu Houze, culture minister Wang Meng and with a number of free-thinking journalists who were subsequently dismissed from the party for their activities during November and December, and he was seen as an initial supporter and instigator of the 'Democracy Movement'. His ineffective actions during December 1986 and his overly liberal musings on the future extent of political reform during the preceding months had forfeited him the support of his patron Deng, who, while favouring a measure of increased political participation and accountability, drew the line at pluralist criticisms of the CPC's paramount role and at departures from 'democratic centralism'. Deng stated bluntly, 'If you are a member of the Chinese Communist Party, you have to accept party orders.' At a specially convened meeting of his closest aides — Hu Yaobang, Zhao Ziyang, Wan Li and Hu Qili — on 30 December 1986, Deng severely reprimanded Hu for his failure to prevent the student protests from spreading and called upon him to tender his resignation. Hu, after initially refusing, finally agreed to step down as party leader at an enlarged Politbureau meeting on 16 January

1987.[1] In his parting speech Hu, while contesting a number of the charges made against him, admitted that his errors had been 'serious' and had caused 'grave damage to the party and people' and apologised for failing to honour the 'mission' confided in him by the CPC and also for disappointing the expectations of 'the people, the party and the older generation of leaders'.

The resignation of Hu, Deng Xiaoping's closest and longest serving aide, came as a serious blow to supporters of the post-1978 liberalisation programme and appeared to place Deng's continued dominance as China's 'paramount ruler' in jeopardy. Deng tried to minimise the damage and disruption to his reform programme by successfully securing the election of Zhao Ziyang as the temporary new party leader at the Politbureau meeting of 16 January.[2] In addition, Deng moved quickly to distance himself publicly from the political reformism of Hu Yaobang, documents being leaked during February 1987 which suggested that Deng had been in disagreement with Hu for a number of years over the extent of reform to be tolerated. A judicious new collection of speeches by Deng was also now published in which he was depicted as a staunch advocate of 'democratic centralism' and of a more orthodox ideological approach.

However, despite these nimble moves, Deng Xiaoping could not forestall a sharp conservative lurch in policy attitudes during the early months of 1987 as a crackdown on intellectual dissent was launched under the supervision of the new hardline CPC propaganda secretary Wang Rezhi, who had replaced the dismissed Zhu Houze. This new anti-intellectual and anti-rightist campaign resulted in the arrest and dismissal from the CPC of a number of prominent writers and civil rights campaigners.[3] It

---

[1] The Politbureau was enlarged to include senior conservatives from the CAC.

[2] Zhao retained his post as State Premier, agreeing to serve in both posts until new elections for the party leadership were effected at the 13th CPC Congress in September-October 1987. A number of Zhao's party leadership functions were, however, informally shared by Deng Xiaoping who became more active on the political stage during 1987.

[3] Those dismissed from their posts and expelled from the CPC included Professor Fang Lizhi, the investigative journalist, Liu Binyan, and the Shanghai writer Wang Ruowang. The presidents of the Hefei Institute of Science and Technology and the China Academy of Sciences were demoted and transferred to new positions, while the dissidents Liu De (a Sichuan University Graduate who had called on the people to 'rise up' and overthrow the CPC) and Shi Guanfu (a Shanghai factory worker who had formed the Weimin Party as an alternative to the CPC) were arrested and jailed for 'counter-revolutionary activity'.

widened into a broader rectification campaign directed against 'spiritual pollution' and 'bourgeois liberalism' (Western ideas) within party, army and state administration ranks. The campaign was led by the revivified figure of Peng Zhen (84), the NPC's Standing Committee Chairman, who began to emerge as a potential new power-broking rival to Deng Xiaoping,[1] and was supported by a clutch of senior party leaders. They included Bo Yibo (84: Chairman of the Central Commission for Guiding Party Rectification), Hu Qiaomu (82), President Li Xiannian (82), Chen Yun (81), Wang Zhen (79), Yu Qiuli (74), Deng Liqun (72) and Yao Yilin (71), as well as the rising young figures of Li Peng and Qiao Shi. The movement involved the re-emphasis of the traditional Maoist virtues of frugalism and self-reliance, a resurgence in nationalistic chauvinism and, above all, a stress on adherence to the 'four cardinal principles'.[2] In the economic sphere, the new swing towards conservatism forced the continued shelving of proposed new deregulationary reforms, the cancellation of a number of foreign contracts and a savage 50% cutback in the capital spending programme as finance minister Wang Bingqian unveiled an 'austerity budget for 1987-8.

The conservative counterblast, however, fell far short of that which had been experienced after June 1957 when the rug was pulled from under the 'Hundred Flowers' movement and a violent anti-rightist purge instituted. Deng Xiaoping and the new CPC leader Zhao Ziyang managed to ensure that 'rectification' was largely confined to within party ranks and repeatedly pledged their continued support for the post-1978 economic reforms and for the maintenance of an 'open door' policy approach. Thus, by the time the NPC convened for its annual two-week session at the end of

[1] Peng Zhen had become NPC Standing Committee Chairman in June 1983 following the retirement of Ye Jianying (who later died, in Ocober 1986) and had rapidly built up the NPC's Standing Committee into a personal power base. The son of a poor Shanxi peasant farmer, Peng had joined the CPC in 1923. He was appointed mayor of Peking in 1949 and rose to become the second-ranking secretary in the CPC's central Secretariat headed by Deng Xiaoping during the 1950s, before being purged during the 'Cultural Revolution'. Peng bore a grudge against Deng for the tardiness of his rehabilitation to office in 1979 and for Deng's failure to promote him to the Standing Committee of the CPC's Politbureau. He enjoyed a reputation as a strictly orthodox adherent to Marxism.

[2] The 'four cardinal principles' comprised: adherence to the 'socialist road', the people's democratic dictatorship, the party leadership, and to Marxist-Leninist-Mao Zedong thought.

March 1987, the 'spiritual pollution' campaign had passed its peak and the Deng-Zhao duumvirate had begun to reassert firmer control over the Chinese polity. The NPC session was deliberately staged in a manner which emphasised party unity. Hu Yaobang had been allowed to retain his membership of the Politbureau Standing Committee and the CPC Central Committee and remained at the centre of Chinese politics, being elected to the NPC's Praesidium and being given substantial press coverage.[1] Hu sat immediately behind Premier Zhao Ziyang as Zhao delivered a two-hour keynote 'state of the nation' speech which formed the centrepiece of the congress. In this important address, Zhao praised the 'bourgeois liberalisation' campaign for curbing dangerous influences which, if left unchecked, would have threatened the nation with chaos and disorder (*luan*). He stated, however that the campaign had achieved its principal aims and would now be wound down, with emphasis being shifted back towards economic regeneration and reform, though at a more sensible and cautious pace than during recent years.

Zhao Ziyang's speech to the NPC represented a skilful and pragmatic balance between reform and conservatism and was reminiscent in style and content of the addresses delivered during the early 1970s by the popular centrist Prime Minister Zhou Enlai. Zhao's astute actions and his rapid consolidation of power during the months following the crisis of January 1987 have significantly improved his standing within the CPC élite and enhanced his prospects of eventually succeeding Deng Xiaoping as the nation's future 'paramount ruler'. However, much will depend upon which party faction, the reformist or the conservative, emerges dominant at the crucial 13th CPC Congress in September-October 1987 and obtains the upper hand in the key elections to the party's new Central Committee and Politbureau. Much will also depend upon how long Deng Xiaoping will be able to postpone his 'meeting with Marx' and thus give Premier Zhao Ziyang more time to strengthen his position as party leader. It also depends upon whether Deng can outlive his 'conservative reformist' rivals Peng Zhen and Chen Yun, both of whom control powerful patronage networks of their own and seek to promote their protégés to power.

However, whether or not Zhao Ziyang succeeds in establishing himself as China's next 'paramount leader', the events of December

---

[1]   The Praesidium of the NPC is a body which is elected to oversee the proceedings of each annual session.

1986 — January 1987 suggest that future room for policy manoeuvre will remain severely circumscribed for whoever governs the country during the next quinquennium. The powerful conservative reaction to the Hefei-Shanghai-Peking reform movement in the winter of 1986 demonstrates the limits that exist to further liberalising and decentralising reform in both the economic and political spheres. Key elements at all levels within the party, state and military bureaucracies remain opposed to such moves and can draw outside support for their views from disadvantaged, particularly urban, workers. However, the 'conservative reformist' grouping centred around Peng Zhen and Chen Yun, who were both fierce critics of the 'Great Leap Forward' and the 'Cultural Revolution', equally opposes a sudden lurch back towards Maoist extremism and supports many aspects of the Dengist reform experiment. In addition, a broader popular constituency, comprising technocrats, intellectuals, successful peasants and skilled workers, would firmly oppose the substantial abandonment of the post-1978 initiatives. A compromise reform strategy, embracing, in particular, Deng's popular rural reforms, while reversing a number of the more recent and less popular urban initiatives and re-exerting tighter central control, thus appears the likely policy course for China's leadership in the foreseeable future. Such a policy strategy might result in a somewhat slower rate of economic growth than was achieved between 1978 and 1986, but it would have the advantage of preserving order and political stability. Its adoption would enhance the party and state leadership prospects of Qiao Shi and Li Peng, the more orthodox representatives of the rising new 'third echelon', to the detriment of the reformists Hu Qili, Tian Jiyun and Li Ruihuan. However, the latter trio, taking note of the change that has taken place in the political climate since January 1987, have recently adopted a more cautious and orthodox policy stance in an effort to retain influence and to continue to play a key role in the shaping of China's future.

Part Three

ECONOMIC AND SOCIAL DEVELOPMENTS

China's Growth Performance 1949-1976: An Overview

China's growth record since 1949 has been fitful and characterised by sudden shifts in policy direction.

The first years (1949-57) after the revolution saw spectacular expansion from a low base. The nation's GNP grew by an average of 8% per annum, with industry averaging 18% and agriculture 4.5%. A moderate mixed economy, popular-front policy was adopted at first, with private industrialists being tolerated and agricultural land remaining in private hands, although it was redistributed towards peasants with smallholdings. Gradually, however, as the CPC's control over Chinese society deepened, a more radical socialist approach to economic development became evident, signalled by the launch of the 'Five Anti' campaign in 1952. The state began to interfere increasingly in the industrial sector, ousting the private capitalist and establishing a central planning system, with priority being given to heavy industry, following the Soviet model. In the rural sector, peasant farmers were encouraged to join together in co-operative farming, using only small portions of their own land for private vegetable growing and poultry rearing.

The ensuing quinquennium (1958-62) was one of initial growth followed by dramatic stagnation as Mao's 'Great Leap Forward' strategy of 'walking on two legs' was introduced. This sought to accelerate growth in the agricultural and light industrial sectors through the establishment of huge communes in which farming would be mechanised and where previously underemployed labour would be used in large infrastructural projects and in small-scale industry. The radical 'Great Leap' programme failed, however, as a result of opposition from the peasantry, problems of co-ordination and chance climatic factors.

The 'Great Leap' communalisation programme was slowly abandoned between 1960-62, with private 'supplementary plots' being restored, communal mess-halls closed and planning reverting to the 'co-operative' level. A moderate and pragmatic 'recovery programme' was then pursued during the next three years by the Liu-Zhou-Deng team which combined a measure of decentralisation in decision-taking with the injection of a number of market disciplines into agriculture and industry. This programme, with the high priority it gave to agricultural investment and its toleration of private farming, accentuated China's divergence form the Soviet model which had first become evident in 1958.

The 1962-65 'recovery programme' boosted China's growth rate and proved to be an economic success. It was, however, abandoned for political and ideological reasons, as Mao embarked on the radical 'Cultural Revolution' and launched the economy into another period of egalitarian extremism. The communes were revived as local economic, social and political units, private plots were outlawed and rural markets closed. In urban areas, factories were taken over by leftist-dominated 'revolutionary committees' and technocrat managers and administrators were attacked and purged. These policies, coupled with civil disorder and the dispersal of millions of Red Guard youths into the countryside, had a baneful influence on China's economic performance in the years between 1966 and 1971.

Another centrist 'recovery programme' was thus introduced by Zhou Enlai and Deng Xiaoping between 1972 and 1976 in which the commune system was once more slowly dismantled and private plots and material incentives restored. Zhou and Deng also gave new prominence to technology and education, in what became known as the 'Four Modernisations' programme. However, the continuing strength of Mao and the 'Gang of Four' prevented the full-scale abandonment of the 1966-71 economic system.

Overall, China registered a GNP growth rate of 5.2% per annum during the years between 1958 and 1976, with agricultural output rising by 2% and industrial output by 9% per annum. After population growth of 2% per annum is taken into account, per capita output increased by 3% per annum during this period. This performance was creditable by the standards of other low-income countries, but less so by the standards of the neighbouring Asian nations of Thailand, Malaysia, Taiwan, South Korea, Singapore and Japan, which share a common Buddhist-Confucian heritage and high demographic densities.[1] China's growth has, however, been irregular, with faster bursts being recorded between 1950-57, 1962-65 and 1972-75.

The growth rate slumped once more between 1976/7 as a result of the Tangshan earthquake and the political succession struggle which followed the death of Chairman Mao. Since 1978, however, there has been acceleration. The nation, under new leadership, embarked upon an ambitious and radical new 'open door' and market-related modernisation programme with the aim of quadrupling production per capita by the year 2000. This new programme and its results will be examined in this section, with attention focusing, first, on agriculture, before turning to the urban-industrial sector.

The Agricultural Sector

The Commune Experiment: 1949-1978

In China more than three-quarters of the population live in rural areas and work on the land, so agricultural growth is crucial to the wellbeing of the entire economy. The agricultural sector needs to provide subsistence and luxury foodstuffs, as well as industrial raw materials and a surplus for export and investment. Years of crop failure have a marked impact upon the industrial sector, on government finances and on political stability.

Mao Zedong, coming from a peasant farming family himself, was acutely aware of agriculture's importance and gave it priority in the post-1958 economic plans. In addition, he framed a new approach to rural development. He believed that China's individualistic system of private smallholding had been a prime factor hindering the country's growth and he encouraged instead the development of large-scale co-operative and collective farming to make the most efficient use of labour and technology. A network of huge collectives and communes was thus established from the mid 1950s, each commune functioning as a centre for farming, infra-structural development and craft and processing industries.

By 1970 there were more than 50 000 communes spread across the Chinese countryside, each comprising a population of 10 000-40 000 and incorporating 30-40 industrial enterprises. They were organisationally subdivided into 'production brigades' composed of 500-2000 peasants, and 'production teams', comprising 50-200

[1]   These neighbouring Asian countries recorded 4.5 — 6.5% annual growth in GNP per capita during the corresponding period.

people. Each commune elected a management committee to oversee the commune's economic, political and social development. It agreed annual production targets with the State Planning Organisation, determined land usage and cropping patterns, organised the maintenance of roads and irrigation channels, financed and oversaw local factories, maintained security grain stores and had responsibility for local health, educational, welfare and political activities. The 'production brigades' and 'production teams' apportioned labour duties between their members, with each worker being paid out of production team profits on the basis of tasks completed — the 'work-points' system. During years when the CPC pragmatists gained the upper hand in their battle with Mao (i.e. 1962-65 and 1972-76), decision-making authority devolved down from the commune management committee to the brigade and team levels.

The commune system was later to be roundly condemned by the Deng-Hu-Zhao triumvirate for stultifying peasant initiative. However, during its years of operation between 1958 and 1976, a significant number of benefits did flow from the new system. Numerous large-scale irrigation, road construction and soil reclamation projects were carried out using directed commune labour during the slack winter months. Investment was also made in modern processing equipment and farm machinery, including tractors, which could be operated with the benefit of economies of scale. Finally, the commune was able to provide welfare facilities efficiently and economically for young and old, and to free able-bodied women from domestic duties, so enabling them to take up productive employment in the fields. These advantages, coupled with the increased use of fertilisers and high-yielding seeds and the shift to more intensive cropping and tillage systems, enabled Chinese agriculture to increase overall production by 2% per annum between 1958 and 1976; 100 million additional workers were absorbed; and the number of days worked per person rose from 160 to 250 per annum.[1]

During this period, the increase in agricultural output rose at a pace just ahead of that for population and the improved distribution of foodstuffs enabled China to avoid serious famine (excepting the years 1959-62), improve the quality of the diet and raise life expectancy. However, agriculture's performance remained disappointing when compared to that of the industrial

[1] The Chinese agricultural workforce rose from 243 million to 342 million between these dates.

sector and continued to act as a brake on the rest of the Chinese economy. This made the post-Mao leadership anxious to find new ways of accelerating agricultural growth.

Hua Guofeng and his moderate Maoist supporters saw the solution to the 'agricultural question' to be one of increased mechanisation in a commune setting, with Dazhai, the successful commune established by Chen Yongkui in Shanxi province, being regarded as a model to be emulated. This 'extensivist' approach was rejected, however, by Deng Xiaoping, the eventual victor in the post-Mao succession battle, who favoured radical structural reform and the dismemberment of the commune system.

Deng's 'Responsibility System': 1978-1987

Deng placed agriculture top of his list of the 'Four Modernisations'. However, he sought to stimulate its growth not by throwing scarce resources into mechanisation, but through stimulating individual peasant initiative and intensifying production. He believed that, given incentives, peasant farmers producing for themselves would work harder and prove to be more efficient than when directed by commune teams and paid through the 'work-points system'. Deng did not support the idea of untrammelled free-market private enterprise, but he saw a place for individual production within the framework of a broad strategic and party-controlled plan. Deng first experimented with these ideas during the 1962-65 recovery programme when he introduced the 'guarantee system', allowing peasants to farm land in families or small groups if they, in return undertook to deliver fixed quotas of produce to the state. This scheme was abolished during the 'Cultural Revolution', but it was resurrected in a modified form once Deng was established in power in 1978 in what became a major departure in China's agrarian policy.

Deng's reform strategy was two-pronged: organisational and economic. He sought, firstly, to dismantle the rigid, bureaucratic controls of the commune system, giving greater decision-making responsibility to work team and family units, and, secondly, to stimulate production through raising price returns to cultivators.

Organisation Reform The earliest reform initiatives were effected in Sichuan in 1977 by the province's 1st Party Secretary Zhao Ziyang. Zhao transferred political and economic power from the communes to the old town and village authorities in three counties and turned enterprises which had previously been run by the communes into joint stock companies, paying brigades and the commune an annual dividend. This example was swiftly followed in Anhui in east-central China by 1st Party Secretary Wan Li, a man brought into the Secretariat in February 1980.

The downgrading and dismantling of the commune system became progressive throughout China from 1979 as the use of what became known as the 'responsibility' or 'contract' (*zhiren zhi*) system spread. In this system, 'production teams' contracted to supply a stipulated amount of produce at a fixed price and were then allowed to consume or sell any surplus produced and have full control over planting on the remainder of their cultivated area. They continued to pay, in addition, welfare contributions into a collective fund. In poor agricultural regions the scheme operated differently. Contractual responsibility was devolved down to the individual family level in what was known as the 'household responsibility system'. This more radical system was extended to more prosperous regions after 1982 and became the norm over more than half of China's cultivated area.

Two additional significant concessions were made after 1982. First, in an effort to encourage private investment, the land contracted to farmers began to be granted on hereditary leases to peasant families for periods of up to 30 years, in what became a new system of state landlordism.[1] Secondly, a number of former commune workers (10-15% of the total) were given dispensation to establish themselves as 'specialised households', turning what had previously been sideline activities, such as poultry rearing, processing or craftwork, into a full-time occupation organised on modern, professional lines.

Price Reform Besides these organisational changes, Deng also markedly raised the prices paid to farmers for crops they produced in an effort to stimulate production. Major hikes in the purchase prices for all agricultural products were effected during the years between 1978 and 1984 and a two-track pricing schedule was introduced for grains, with the state agreeing to pay higher rates for any crops produced in excess of the quota level. Urban consumers were shielded from the full effects of these producer price increases through an expensive system of government subsidies.

Deng sought, thirdly, to stimulate agricultural production through the injection of investment capital. This proved, however,

[1] Lessees, when surrendering land, would be compensated for any improvements made.

to be a less important element of the rural development programme than the 'responsibility system' and price reform initiative. In 1980 the agricultural sector still received only 14% of state investment capital compared to heavy industry's 46%.

The Response to Deng's Rural Reform Programme

China's peasants, remembering well the sudden changes in policy direction that had taken place during the years between 1958 and 1976, acted at first with understandable caution. However, as the 'responsibility system' became firmly established their response became spectacular. China's agricultural output increased at a rate of 8% per annum during the period 1978-85;[1] grain production rose by a third (see Table 8), rendering the country self-sufficient; wheat and cash-crop output increased by two-thirds; and vegetable, meat and poultry production by an even higher proportion. The increased use of fertiliser and new 'Green Revolution' wonder seeds was one factor behind the improvement in gross output and yields during these years. The prime factor was, however, the intensification of labour inputs by peasant family farms.

TABLE 8: China's Grain Production, 1956-1985 (Million Tonnes)

	1956-60	1961-65	1966-70	1971-75	1976-80	1981-85
Average per annum	176.6	184.8	225.0	262.2	305.2	370.4

	1976	1977	1978	1979	1980	1981	1982	1983	1984	1985
Grain Harvest	285	283	305	337	316	325	353	387	407	379

The reward for China's cultivators was a doubling in farm incomes between 1978 and 1985 to a level of 350 *yuan* (£120) per annum and the filtering into the countryside of a number of minor luxuries. The rise in farm incomes, although they still remained

---

[1] This rate was in excess of Hua Guofeng's seemingly ambitious target of 4.5% per annum announced in his 1976-85 Ten Year Plan.

extraordinarily low by international standards, gave a significant stimulus to rural service, house construction and manufacturing industries and to the development of small market towns. This set off a virtuous spiral of growth, creating new employment in non-agricultural professions.[1]

Deng Xiaoping was understandably heartened by the success of his agricultural reforms. Other, more conservative, members of the CPC élite were, however, vexed by a number of the side-effects of the new rural programme.

Maoist traditionalists disliked the weakening of party control, the diminishing emphasis on political education and the growing neglect of local welfare institutions which had resulted from the dismemberment of the communes. They were appalled, in addition, by the re-emergence of a new selfish and acquisitive 'rich peasant' élite and by the widening of rural income differentials which had resulted from the encouragement of individual initiative and the overzealous early official injunctions to 'get rich quick'. They feared a recrudescence of rural class conflict.

More moderate critics of Deng's rural reform programme were worried by three other adverse developments. Firstly, the return to individual family farming had led to the neglect of infrastructural projects and had prevented the economical use of farm machinery. Repairs to village irrigation systems were no longer carried out, while many tractors were standing idle. The neglect of the irrigation systems promised to have serious long-term repercussions for agricultural output. It was particularly serious in the 'dry villages' of north-eastern China. In this wheat and millet-growing region, which included Dazhai village, large irrigation and hill terrace networks had previously been built and repaired by 'free' winter labour in a commune system which had been of particular value. Secondly, the government's efforts to encourage grain production through special price, fertiliser and input concessions produced an unsatisfactory consequence. The higher returns which peasant farmers received from intensive cash crop production and 'sideline' ventures, coupled with growing regional cropping specialisation and burgeoning consumer demand for 'luxury' foodstuffs, had

---

[1] The numbers employed in agricultural fieldwork actually began to fall in this period as a result of the stimulus given to non-agricultural activities. Up to 50 million people moved wholly or partly into rural industry between 1980-5. This trend seems set to continue, with China's planners projecting a doubling in the size of the non-agricultural population between 1985 and the year 2000.

resulted in a steady decline in the cultivated area sown with grain. The proportion fell from 80% of the total in 1980 to 75.6% in 1985. This decline in the sown area did not affect gross output between 1980 and 1984 since grain yields rose at a faster pace. It did, however, affect output in 1985, when serious floods and droughts in the interior provinces depressed yields and caused a 7% fall in total grain production. This alarmed Deng's moderate critics, including Chen Yun, who predicted a serious future food crisis unless policies were markedly adjusted.[1] Thirdly, the rising cost of agricultural price subsidies, reaching a figure of Rmb. 20 billion (equivalent to 20% of the state budget), was causing severe fiscal problems for the central government.

At the heart of the varied criticism of Deng's rural reforms has been the suspicion that much of its success would be only short-term and that diminishing returns would result as the infrastructure bequeathed by the commune system slowly crumbled and as assets, such as cattle, were sold and slaughtered for profit at too rapid a rate. In addition, it has been felt that, like Mao's communalisation programme, Deng's reform programme has been introduced in too rigid and doctrinaire a manner, giving too little regard to local agricultural conditions. It proved to be more suited to the intensive rice-growing tracts of southern China, whose infrastructural needs were smaller in scale, than to the drier northern and western portions of the country.

Deng took some note of these criticisms in 1985 when he framed the 1986-90 Five Year Plan. In this plan the projected pace of agricultural growth was slowed to 7% per annum and emphasis was placed upon the need for greater co-operation in farming and new incentives were introduced to encourage grain cultivation. In addition, the price levels for non-grain agricultural produce were frozen in 1985/6. However, such is the popularity of Deng's reforms among China's rural population that it appears likely that their broad principles will be maintained during the foreseeable future. Only minor adjustments will be made in an effort to bring about a truer union between private and corporate initiative.

---

[1] A similar shift within the cultivated area from grains to cash crops was experienced during the 1962-65 'recovery programme' and led to a rising level of grain imports. This was remedied during the 'Cultural Revolution' when priority was given to grain cultivation — the 'key link'. A decline in the proportion of the cultivated area sown under grains for human consumption appears inevitable, however, during the 1990s as a result of rising demand for meat and luxury foodstuffs as income levels improve.

The Urban and Industrial Sector

From the 'Stalinist Model' to the 'Four Modernisations': 1949-1976

The industrial sector was given top priority by the CPC leadership during China's initial post-revolution decade. Growth in industry, it was believed, would provide jobs for the burgeoning rural population and would slowly but surely transform China into a modern, urban-based socialist nation. The Stalinist development model was closely adhered to in China's first Five Year Plan (1953-57), with resources being concentrated upon infrastructural and heavy industry projects and with peasant incomes being tightly squeezed: 30% of the GNP being reinvested during this period. But hopes of a rapid transition from agriculture to industry began to fade during the late 1950s. This led Mao to develop a unique Chinese development strategy which placed dual emphasis on both agriculture and industry and which encouraged the development of small-scale 'intermediate technologies' in rural areas in an effort to 'industrialise the countryside'. Employment in and movement to urban areas became tightly controlled through the introduction of travel permits and local ration cards and two forms of industry began to develop, the large modern and invariably urban-based 'state enterprises' and the small- to medium-sized, predominantly commune-based, 'collective enterprises'. Official support for the latter form of enterprise reached its peak during the 'Cultural Revolution'.

For much of the period between 1957 and 1976 first priority continued to be given to the development of the modern, heavy-industry sector. This led to impressive sectoral achievements, with major steel, coal, oil, electricity and construction industries being established (see Table 9) and a nuclear capability being reached in 1964. The overall industrial growth rate during this period was 9% per annum, with a higher rate for the heavy industry sector, which grew ninety-fold between 1949-78 compared with a twenty-fold expansion of light industry. These rapid rates of industrial growth helped to create 50 million new urban jobs, bringing the total to 88 million. However, such was the pace of contemporary rural demographic growth that little real impact was made on urbanisation levels, which rose only from 18% to 21%. China needed to run just to stand still.

TABLE 9: China's Industrial Production 1952-1985 (Million Tonnes)

	1952	1961	1970	1976	1985
Oil	0.4	5.3	28.5	83.6	125.0
Coal	66.5	170.0	310.0	448.0	850.0
Steel	1.4	8.0	17.8	23.0	46.7
Cement	2.9	8.0	19.8	37.3	84.0[1]
Fertiliser	0.2	1.8	2.8	5.5	13.5[1]
Cloth (bn metres)	3.8	3.3	7.5	7.6	14.3[1]
Electricity (bn kWh)	7.3	31.0	72.0	124.0	351.0[1]

[1] 1983 figure

It was against this background that Premier Zhou Enlai, in tandem with Deng Xiaoping, launched the ambitious 'Four Modernisations' programme in 1975. This envisaged a rapid acceleration of both agricultural and industrial growth rates and a quadrupling of national output by the year 2000, at which date China would, it was hoped, have emerged as a fully modern industrial power comparable with any in the West.

The 'Four Modernisations' under Hua and Deng: 1976-1987

The need for modernisation appeared to be accepted by both Mao Zedong and his protégé and immediate successor Hua Guofeng during the years between 1975 and 1978. However, they interpreted the scheme differently from Zhou and Deng. Hua, in implementing the 'Four Modernisations', sought to adhere to the orthodox Maoist principles of tight party control and communal methods of production. He introduced an ambitious Ten Year Plan (a 'new Long March') in February 1978 to cover the period between 1976 and 1985. This envisaged industrial growth of 10% per annum, agricultural growth of 4.5% per annum and the construction of 120 large-scale industrial and infrastructural complexes. This plan recalled the ambitious Twelve Year Plan introduced by Mao Zedong during the mid 1950s preceding the 'Great Leap Forward'. It relied on mechanisation and moral exhortations, rather than on structural change, improved efficiency and material incentives for the fulfilment of its objectives.

Zhou and his protégé Deng Xiaoping interpreted the 'Four Modernisations' programme differently. For them it entailed firstly, the creation of a better skilled, trained and educated workforce and

81

management which would be selected on the basis of expertise and ability rather than political belief. Secondly, it involved opening up China to foreign investment, markets and suppliers. Thirdly, it entailed a decentralisation of decision-making authority to managers and workers and a curb on stifling bureaucratic interference. Finally, it entailed, for Deng, a willingness to inject market forces into the economy to encourage greater efficiency at the enterprise level and to reward skill, industry and initiative by means of incentives. Taken together, and to their Dengist extreme, this policy programme marked a major departure from the Maoist development model.

The first element of this policy programme to be implemented was that of educational reform. Zhou Enlai sought during his final years in office to repair the damage inflicted to the educational sector by the 'Cultural Revolution's' anti-intellectual and rustication campaigns. He fought for the reintroduction of the examination system, which had been abandoned in 1966, and the injection of increased resources to improve standards and expand the numbers attending schools and universities. His reform programme was blocked, at first, by the 'Gang of Four' in 1975/6, but it was ultimately implemented by the Hua and Deng administrations. School examinations were reintroduced in 1977, universal ten-year schooling was established by 1985 and plans were set in train to double the intake of higher education institutes by 1990, giving particular emphasis to scientific, technical and commercial education. These reforms had already made a significant impact by 1985 and had begun to produce new technocrat managers and party cadres who would be required to take China into the 21st century.

The transformation in China's external commercial relations after 1978 was even more striking as the new CPC leadership embarked upon a radically new 'open door' strategy. During the 1950s China had drawn on substantial Soviet technical and economic aid, but for the remainder of the Mao era the nation had sought self-reliance and self-sufficiency in an insular and autarchic manner. This strategy was feasible in a country the size of China, endowed with huge energy and mineral reserves. It served, nonetheless, to hinder the pace of economic growth. Recognising this, Zhou Enlai and Deng Xiaoping pressed, during the early 1970s, for a relaxation in China's commercial controls and an opening up of the country to the outside world. They believed that China should draw in capital from abroad and import advanced Western technology as a means of boosting the industrial growth rate. These technology imports could, they believed, be paid for through raising China's exports of oil and textiles and through developing new higher technology and consumer-goods export lines, utilising the nation's cheap labour supplies following the example set by neighbouring Asian countries.

During the early stages of this new policy shift, diplomatic contacts were re-established with the West through the determined efforts of Zhou Enlai and his foreign ministry team. This diplomatic offensive culminated in the normalisation of relations with the United States in December 1978. (See Part 4). Once such contacts had been effected, China's commerce and industry ministers were sent off around Europe, America and the Pacific Basin on 'shopping expeditions', signing new trade agreements and arranging for the purchase of modern machinery for the country's new steel mills, coal mines, oil fields and chemical factories. They were particularly active between 1977-81 and 1983-85. China's imports increased more than sixfold, between 1977 and 1985 (see Table 10), to $43 billion, with Japan and Germany emerging as the major trading partners.[1] Indirect foreign credits and loans, including 'soft loans' from the World Bank, which China joined in 1980, helped to pay for some of these purchases.

TABLE 10 : China's Foreign Trade 1956-1985 ($ bn)						
	1956-60	1961-65	1966-70	1971-75	1976-80	1981-85
Imports	1.8	1.4	2.0	4.2	12.1	25.7
Exports	1.9	1.8	2.1	4.1	11.9	23.3

A second and even more dramatic development in China's commercial policy occurred in 1979, when four south-eastern coastal towns were designated 'Special Economic Zones' (SEZs) into which foreign investment would be attracted on concessionary terms. The Chinese government hoped that these areas would become foci for modern high-technology export industries and it sought to entice foreign investors with the prospect of free land and building equipment, low-cost labour, the exemption of duties on

[1] In 1984 30% of China's imports came from Japan, 15% from the United States, 10% from Hong Kong and 6% from West Germany. Of China's exports 27% were sent to Hong Kong, 22% to Japan, 10% to the United States, 4% to Singapore and 3% to West Germany.

imported raw materials and equipment and the grant of an initial two to four years' tax-free operation before subsequent taxation at a concessionary rate of 15%. A number of these privileges were extended to 14 other coastal cities in 1984 (see Figure 4), which were to form a modern network of capitalist 'Treaty Port' enclaves.

These changes did not, however, suddenly transform China into an 'open economy' on the Western model. Extensive import and tariff controls remained in place to insulate China's domestic market to such a degree that external trade still accounted for only 5-10% of the nation's GNP. In addition, these reforms did not work as smoothly as was first envisaged. Overseas firms, unconvinced as to the permanence of the country's new policy line, proved wary of investing in the new SEZs. Foreign investment in China thus remained disappointing. For the period between 1979-85, it totalled less than $4.6 billion, $1 billion of which was consumed in offshore oil prospecting and much of the remainder represented the capital of Hong Kong entrepreneurs who had moved their operations across the border.[1] Of the SEZs only Shenzhen, situated adjacent to Hong Kong, attracted significant capital and even this sum barely repaid the amount the Chinese government had spent on local infrastructural development. This paucity of foreign investment, coupled with the quota restrictions which blocked China's textile shipments to Europe and America,[2] meant that the nation's exports of manufactured items failed to increase at a fast enough pace to pay for its growing technology imports. The result was a dangerous widening in China's trade deficit between 1978-80 and 1984/5. The figure reached $14 billion in 1985, and a series of currency crises forced sharp cutbacks in the nation's modernisation programme in 1981/2 and in 1986.

The boost that the Chinese economy gained from its new 'open door' policy had proved, by 1986, to be less substantial than anticipated. Technology imports from the West did help to increase the country's production of coal, steel, chemicals and fertiliser. while the import of consumer goods from Japan improved the living standards of the urban 'middle classes'. But the growth in imports created serious fiscal problems and fostered public unrest,

[1] A further $11 billion was planned in 29 000 projected schemes. Many of these, however, were orientated towards China's internal market.

[2] These restrictions persuaded China to apply to join GATT in 1986 in an attempt to negotiate improved trading terms.

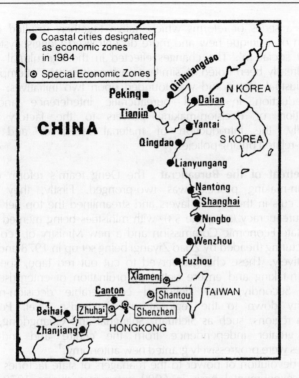

FIGURE 4
China's Special Economic Zones and Designated Coastal Cities

while the SEZ experiment bred a series of debilitating corruption scandals (see page 56). With these disappointing returns, it was not surprising that in 1986 the Chinese government began to take a more cautious attitude to overseas commerce and investment and to impose more stringent tariff restrictions.

At the heart of the change in direction in China's economic policy after 1978 was reform of the domestic economy. The Deng-Hu-Zhao team believed that major structural changes were essential if the Chinese economy was to grow at a faster pace during the remaining two decades of the century. They rejected Hua Guofeng's attempt, in the 1976-85 Ten Year Plan, to achieve rapid growth within the framework of the Maoist system and introduced instead a series of reforms which, taken together, resulted in the creation of a unique new and more decentralised Dengist system of 'market socialism'. The changes effected in the agricultural sector have already been noted. A similar transformation was attempted in the industrial sector and was founded upon two initiatives: firstly, the reduction in central bureaucratic interference and the devolution of decision-making powers to the factory level; secondly, the introduction of material incentives and more market-related pricing policies.

The Retreat of the Bureaucrat The Deng team's reform of the decision-making process was two-pronged. Firstly, they made savage cuts in the middle layers and streamlined the top tier of the state bureaucracy (see page 53), with ministries being merged and a new State Economic Commission and a new Ministry of Economic Restructuring (headed by Zhao Ziyang) being set up in 1978 and 1982 respectively. These changes served to cut out red tape, speed up decision-taking and ensure better co-ordination of enterprises and plans. Secondly, they devolved considerable decision-making authority down to the regional and enterprise level. Potential growth regions, such as Sichuan, Shanghai and Guangdong, were given greater independence from the centre and individual factories were progressively granted new autonomy.[1]

The devolution of power to the managers of state factories began on an experimental basis in 6000 enterprises during 1979. Each factory was given a procurement and production target, but, once this was met, the management was left free to adjust its output to market demand as necessary. In addition, enterprises were allowed to retain a share of their surplus profits and to purchase raw material inputs from any supplier. They were even empowered to deal directly with foreign buyers. The state, in an effort to encourage greater awareness of 'real costs', charged in return a fee for any investment funds it provided. This scheme was gradually extended to a further 80 000 'state enterprises' during the years after 1981, being concentrated particularly in the light industry sector.

In October 1984 even greater powers were extended to 'state enterprises. The CPC General Committee launched a major new 'enterprise management' reform programme for the urban and industrial sector. During a three- to five-year transitional period more than half of the 'state enterprises' were to be granted new

[1] From 1978, provinces were allowed to spend locally the receipts from an increased number of taxes.

autonomy in planning, budgeting and wages and would become directly responsible for their profits and losses. Their prices would become market-related, they would make their own supply and sales deals, they would effect loans from the State Bank and there would be contracted 'responsibility systems' for a number of firms, following the example set in the agricultural sector. Taxes would be repaid to the state on profits made, and companies would become liable to closure if they remained unproductive for a significant period. These firms would be staffed by a new breed of skilled, self-confident and market-conscious managers.

These reforms were designed to affect all firms outside the 'commanding heights' of the economy.[1] Companies in that sector remained, by contrast, under firm central control. They thus saw the CPC reverting to an indirect guiding role, operating through tax and interest rate adjustments, for a major portion of the economy.[2]

The Return of the Market Umbilically connected to this devolution of decision-making responsibility to enterprise managers was the reintroduction of market forces and material incentives into the operation of the economy, in an effort to overcome Chinese industry's curse of low labour productivity and its notoriously inefficient and wasteful use of raw materials, including energy. The reform of the price structure took place at the same time as the 'enterprise management' reforms noted above, with the prices of almost half the country's manufactured items being either deregulated or left to float within broad limits as a result of the October 1984 policy programme.

The reform of the wage system preceded this measure. Industrial workers were encouraged to work harder through being given enhanced wages — receiving their first major rise since 1958 in 1977 — and through the introduction of a system of productivity bonuses and penalties to supplement basic pay, which continued to be regulated by the state. This higher pay was made transferable into improved living standards through the new priority which was given to the expansion of the light industrial, consumer goods

[1] The 'commanding heights' included the heavy industries of steel and engineering, the energy industries of oil, coal and gas, and basic industries such as cigarette manufacture.

[2] This included the 1.5 million small 'collective enterprises' operating in rural areas, which were freed from commune management-committee control and which now operated as independent, competitive firms.

sector in the post-1979 economic plans. In addition, the rigid state and party control of the labour market, with its guarantee of a job for life in what became known as the 'iron rice bowl', was tentatively weakened. The *danwei* (workplace) job assignment system became more flexible, as an effort was made to ensure that the skills of those leaving middle schools and universities were not neglected; factory poaching of technical personnel began to spread; and pressure began to mount to give managers the power to dismiss lazy and incompetent workers.

Taken in combination, these reforms represented the most significant move away from the Moscow model attempted by any contemporary communist nation outside of Yugoslavia, from which country, with its unique factory 'self-management' system, China drew many of its new ideas. Central planning and one-party control still remained and the prices of many basic items such as fuel, steel, housing and essential foodstuffs were controlled or subsidised. In the small firm and light industrial sector, however, a new form of 'market socialism' was established in a more radical fashion than had even been attempted in Hungary.

The Response to Deng's Urban and Industrial Reform Programme

On the face of it, the Deng reform programme appears to have had considerable success. Industrial output and GNP grew by 10% per annum between 1978-85, with the output of many key items rising at an even faster rate (see Tables 9 and 11). However, from a longer-term perspective, the performance of the industrial sector has been less impressive than the agricultural one, with the growth in labour productivity being particularly disappointing. Industry has proved to be a far more complex and onerous sector to stimulate than agriculture. It has been more difficult to build in meaningful incentives and to sort out balances between supply and demand in all stages of production. Serious bottlenecks have thus developed, for example, in the supply of energy and raw materials and in transportation, resulting in a tremendous waste of resources. Substantial year-to-year fluctuations in output have also been recorded in both the heavy and light industry sectors, with planned targets being regularly exceeded by huge amounts. Particularly troublesome has been heavy industry, which is a centre for Maoist cadres. It has consistently spent and grown ahead of budget. In 1982, for example, its projected rate of growth was to be

Politics in China

1%; in fact the actual figure reached 10%. This failure to adhere to planning targets, coupled with the waste of resources, helped to create serious budget deficits and to stoke inflation, particularly between 1979/80 and again in 1985-

TABLE 11 : China's Industrial Performance 1966-1985

	1966-70 %	1971-75 %	1976-80 %	1981-85 %	1986-90 %
GNP Growth	7.2	5.5	8.6	11.1	7.0 (projected)
Ind. Growth	10.0	10.0	9.5	11.0	7.0 (projected)

	1978 %	1979 %	1980 %	1981 %	1982 %	1983 %	1984 %	1985 %
Agr. Growth	9.0	8.5	4.0	7.0	11.0	9.5	16.0	10.0
Ind. Growth	13.0	8.0	9.0	4.5	8.0	10.5	14.0	17.0
Heavy Ind.	NA	7.5	1.5	−5.0	10.0	13.0	12.5	NA
Light Ind.	NA	9.0	18.0	12.0	5.5	8.5	8.5	NA

NA = not available

The reform package has nevertheless brought, on balance, considerable material benefits to China's urban workers. A minority have seen their position deteriorate as a result of unemployment or widening regional and social income differentials. For the majority, though, real incomes have risen substantially. This has been reflected by increased spending on clothing and consumer durables and by improvements in diets, with more meat and poultry now being consumed. It should be noted, however, that much of this rise in consumption standards has been artificially generated rather than earned through productivity improvements. It has been financed through a fiscal boost to the economy which has led to soaring government debt and through costly state subsidies of food, fuel and other basic items, the removal of which would cause great popular anxieties.

The Deng team's domestic economic reforms have now reached a difficult and uncharted stage, with the economy straddled between 'state socialism' and 'market capitalism'. Problems of retaining economic and political control over the Chinese

[1] Inflation reached 7.5% and the budget deficit $17 billion in 1980.

89

economy and society mount for the CPC leadership as it slowly begins to dismantle the full panoply of state and party controls which were erected between 1949-76. Equally, however, the continuance of these controls serves to inhibit enterprise and efficiency and retard growth rates, particularly in the industrial sector. On present rates of growth, China is well on course to meet its goal of quadrupling national income by the year 2000, a task which requires an annual GNP growth rate of 7.2% per annum. There is thus room for the party leadership to decelerate temporarily the pace of reform and to restore firmer central party and state control over both the agricultural and industrial sectors. This is, in fact, occurring under the new 7th Five Year Plan (1986-90), which has sought to rein back growth rates, give greater priority to the traditional heavy industry, energy and infrastructural sectors and to delay implementation of the ambitious October 1984 urban reform programme. Such compromises and pragmatism are essential if the country is to avoid the chaos and disorder that appear likely from pursuing too reckless a dash down the 'capitalist road'.

Future Constraints on Growth: The Population and Energy Questions

Although China remains on course to meet its 1980-2000 goals for growth, two obstacles may still thwart its aims to raise substantially per capita living standards and to continue along the path of modernisation and industrialisation after the year 2000. These are progressive growth in the nation's population base and increased difficulties in satisfying energy needs.

Population Problems: The Land of a Billion

The size and density of China's population have created severe problems for the country's rulers for several centuries, depressing consumption standards and preventing a full transition from agriculture to industry. Matters grew worse between 1949 and 1980. Improvements in food supplies and medical practices served to substantially reduce mortality rates, leading to the addition of 400 million people on to the country's already crowded soil. A family planning programme was briefly introduced in 1962 in an effort to curb the nation's rising birth rate, but this was disrupted by the 'Cultural Revolution'. Not until 1971, when Zhou Enlai launched a major population control programme, promoting the idea of later marriages and smaller family sizes, did the CPC begin to seriously tackle the population question.

The post-Mao leadership has given even greater priority to population control measures. The lead was taken, as in other policy areas, by Zhao Ziyang in innovative Sichuan province with the introduction of a radical new 'one-child family scheme' in 1979. This scheme was subsequently adopted on a national level with the goal of keeping China's population under 1.2 billion by the year 2000 and aiming for a total of 700 million by the year 2080. It involved a mixture of economic inducements — preference in housing, education, employment and free medical care for one-child families, in addition to the grant of a child benefit allowance — and penalties, as well as social and administrative pressure, including, sometimes, physical coercion.

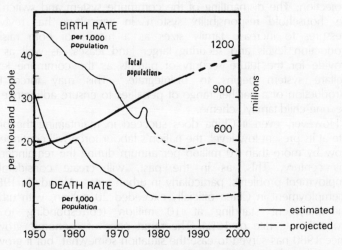

FIGURE 5: China's Demographic Trends 1950-2000

The post-1971 population control campaigns have been remarkably successful. China's overall population growth rate has fallen between 1965 and 1985 by almost 50% to 1.0–1.4% per annum, while the birth rate has fallen by 60%. (See Figure 5.) This birth rate decline was the steepest recorded in the world during this period, with only communist Cuba, at 50%, approaching the figure. There have been a number of adverse side-effects to the birth control campaign. There has, for example, been a revival in female infanticide as families have concentrated upon raising a male heir. In general, though, the programme has been implemented smoothly and with only limited opposition. It has worked well for two principal reasons. Firstly, the high standard of health services provided at the local level in China has fostered life expectancy rates which approach Western levels. This has meant that parents feel confident in limiting family sizes. Secondly, the commune form of organisation, which was in operation until 1980, provided old age security facilities for family elders, reducing the need of parents to look to their offspring for support in later life and provided, in addition, direct social pressure from 'work team' colleagues who stood to be penalised if a family breached the one-child norm.

If the 1971-80 growth trend is maintained China will remain on course to meet its target of a population of only 1.2 billion by the year 2000.[1] One factor has, however, recently begun to disturb this projection. The dismantling of the commune system and switch to the 'household responsibility system' in agriculture has revived pressures to increase family sizes as a means of both raising production levels and securing larger land leases, as well as to provide for the future security of parents as the commune level welfare system begins to disintegrate.[2] This may force the introduction of a harsher range of penalties to ensure adherence to the 'one-child family' scheme.

However, even if China does succeed in maintaining the birth rate at its present low level, the nation's labour force will continue to grow by more than 10 million per annum during the remainder of this century. This, as in the past, will create considerable employment problems, particularly in urban areas. Already in 1980, unemployment in China officially exceeded 20 million, with urban unemployment standing at 10 million (corresponding to a proportionate rate of 10%). The rapid pace of economic growth since 1980 has served to ease the situation somewhat, but if growth rates fall in the 1990s unemployment levels will again rise. China's government, aware of this problem, has begun to encourage people to take up employment in the small-firm service sector, a

[1] As China's birth rate falls and life expectancy rates improve so the nation's age structure will change in an upward direction. By the year 2000 a tenth of the population will be over the age of 60, and by the year 2025 one-fifth. This will have important social spending implications.

[2] Thus in 1984 China's population grew by 11 million at a rate of increase of 10.8 per 1000. In 1986 the country's population grew by 14 million, a rate of increase of 14 per 1000.

sector which remains unusually small by international standards. This employment shift towards the service sector will continue in future years and will serve to create a more mixed and balanced economy.

Energy Developments: Onshore and Offshore

China possesses huge energy resources in the form of coal, oil and gas, but also a rapidly growing appetite for fuel, as the industrial sector expands and as domestic consumption levels rise. It is thus vital for China to continue to expand its energy output during the remainder of the century. The energy sector has therefore received high priority in recent economic plans. A special co-ordinating Energy Commission was established in 1980 and investment has been raised. The long-term aim is to double oil and coal production by the year 2000 in order to provide for both home demand as well as to bring in vital foreign exchange earnings.

Coal forms the mainstay of China's energy resources providing over 70% of its fuel needs. It is to be found in four main fields (see Figure 6): in the north-east, in Shanxi-Shaanxi and Sichuan in Central China and in Xinjiang province in the far west of the country. The oldest fields are in the north-east, but it is the fields of Shaanxi-Shanxi, Sichuan and Xinjiang that production is now expanding at the fastest rate. The Shaanxi-Shanxi fields at present account for 20% of the total Chinese coal output and hold a third of the country's proven coal reserves of 200 billion tonnes. They are, in particular, becoming the centre for the most intensive production and exploration activity.[1] This has sometimes taken place in co-operation with overseas mining companies, who have provided expertise and modern technology.

The development of China's oil resources commenced during the 1950s, when, with Russian aid, the oilfields of Karamay and Urumqi in far western Xinjiang were brought onstream. During the 1960s and early 1970s oil also began to be produced in the north-east at Daqing and in Hebei province at Dagang. This enabled the country to become self-sufficient in oil and to begin exporting surplus production to Japan, bringing in vital foreign exchange.[2] China's oil sector boomed between 1965 and 1979, with output

[1] Production in remote Xinjiang continues to be hampered by the high cost of transport to China's coastal regions and by the limited carriage facilities available.

[2] Oil exports accounted for almost a quarter of China's total foreign exchange earnings during the 1970s.

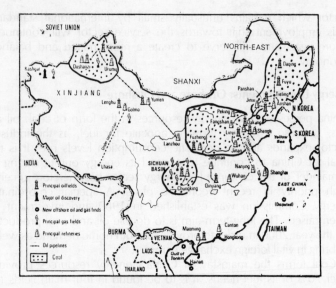

FIGURE 6: China's Energy Resources

rising tenfold to a level of 106 million tonnes per annum. The 1980s, though, have been a less buoyant period.

The important Daqing oilfields, which account for half of the nation's present output, began to run dry during the late 1970s and forced China's energy ministers to accelerate their search for new fields. Considerable reserves still exist onshore in the vicinity of the older fields, and many new wells have recently been opened. It was, however, offshore, where reserves of more than 5 million tonnes were believed to exist, that the attention of ministers particularly turned. Between 1979 and 1983 numerous exploration and drilling agreements were signed with foreign oil companies in an effort to bring offshore oil onstream by the mid 1980s. The preliminary searches proved, however, to be barren and, with falling world oil prices, the enthusiasm of the drilling companies began to wane. This failure to develop the offshore oil reserves resulted in the stagnation in China's gross output between 1980-6. This led, in turn, to fuel shortages for domestic industry and forced the government to begin to restrict its oil exports.

In the medium term, China's energy prospects appear to be promising, with substantial reserves still waiting to be tapped and with the development of hydroelectric and nuclear power being projected.[1] The problem remains, however, of bringing production onstream quickly and economically. Most success has been achieved in expanding coal output (see Table 9), which has persuaded the government to reconvert many oil power stations to coal burning. Another recent success has been the campaign to promote greater fuel efficiency and conservation. Chinese industry is amongst the most profligate consumers of fuel in the world so that great scope lies for economies once Chinese fuel prices are raised close to world market levels. In the short term, though, the energy sector remains a serious bottleneck holding back Chinese industrial production. Fuel shortages have forced more than two-thirds of the country's factories to work below capacity and have led to temporary closures on a rota basis.

Social and Regional Trends: 1976-1987

Despite the nation's commitment to an egalitarian society, social and regional income inequalities continue to exist in communist China, although they are low in comparison with the West or OECD countries. Urban workers earn, on average, more than twice the income of rural workers and are themselves differentiated on a regional, sector and eight-grade occupational basis. The highest paid are those with skills and considerable experience who work in the heavy industry sector in an advanced region such as Shanghai. The lowest paid are young apprentices in the light industrial sector in an interior region. Urban industrial wages vary by a factor of three within one of the nation's eleven 'designated regions' and by a factor of seven on a national basis. Technicians and state administrators are graded separately in a system with 18 and 30 ranks respectively.

In rural areas, peasant cultivators used to be paid a share of the profits of each collective or commune on the basis of their 'work-points' total, with this income being augmented by their 'sideline' earnings from their private allotments. Rural incomes thus varied on a local and regional basis, depending principally on soil fertility

---

[1] In 1980 China announced plans to build ten new nuclear power plants by the year 2000 and to site them principally on the eastern seaboard. These projects have, however, been temporarily shelved in the 7th Five Year Plan as a result of capital constraints. Priority has instead been given to the expansion of coal and hydroelectric power output.

and the proximity of markets. The most prosperous communes were those in the well-watered south and east and those adjacent to towns and communication routes.

Since 1978, the Deng administration's economic reforms have led to a narrowing of rural-urban income differences but a widening of broad social and regional income differentials. In the rural sector, successful 'specialist household' entrepreneurs have emerged as a *nouveau riche* 'rich peasant' élite in the fertile eastern and suburban zones. In the urban sector, skilled workers and managers have benefited in particular, and the east coast seaboard cities in general terms.[1]

A longer-term trend evident, however, in China's economy has been the gradual westward shift in the nation's centre of gravity as the coal, gas, oil, hydroelectric power and iron ore reserves of the central plateau provinces of Sichuan, Shaanxi and Shanxi and the far western province of Xinjiang have been opened up. Important new industries have already been established in these areas, large irrigation canals have been constructed to boost agricultural production and there has been a growing influx of Han Chinese into the traditionally Uyghur and Kazakh-dominated Islamic north-west. In the past, many of these Han Chinese immigrants were drawn from prison camps or had been forced out of east coast cities under the 'rustication campaign'. Increasingly, though, the immigrants are well-educated technicians. They are being freely imported on lucrative contracts in an effort to speed up the development of a region which has been given a high priority in the 7th Five Year Plan. This immigration is disrupting the ethnic balance in the remote and sparsely peopled province of Xinjiang and promises to create friction between the local pastoral community and the urban Han Chinese invaders.

---

[1] It is noticeable that it is from such eastern and southern seaboard provinces that a disproportionate number of the new Dengist political élite are drawn. By contrast, many of the strongest Maoist opponents of the recent reforms are to be found in the poorer interior provinces.

Part Four

DEFENCE AND FOREIGN POLICIES

Tradition, Ideology, Commerce: Influences on Chinese Policy-Making

Communist China's unique approach to foreign affairs has been moulded by an assortment of historical, psychological, ideological, practical and economic influences.

During the Imperial period, the nation's rulers viewed China, the 'Middle Kingdom', as standing at the centre of world civilisation and they displayed a haughty arrogance in their dealings with outside 'barbarian' powers. This feeling of superiority began to erode, however, during the 19th century as the Western powers and neighbouring Japan forced upon the country a series of 'unequal treaties'. A defensive and xenophobic Chinese nationalism developed between 1880 and 1920 in response to these humiliations, emerging most strikingly during the Boxer Rebellion in 1900 and the May 4th Movement in 1919. The new nationalist movement sought the recovery of China's lost rights in the Treaty Port areas, the renegotiation of old 'unequal treaties' and an end to China's dependence upon external powers. Chiang Kai-shek and the Guomindang drew sustenance from this nationalist feeling during the 1920s, but it lost support following Japan's invasion of Manchuria in 1931. It was, instead, the CPC which was to take the lead in the struggle against Japan and to play the key role in the 'liberation war' of 1937-45. The party went on to establish a unique new social order in 1949, which was buttressed by the creation of a confident, new and non-aggressive Chinese nationalism.

China's new communist leaders saw the country possessing clearly defined, historical borders which they would defend through the combination of modern military technology and decentralised, rural-based 'people's warfare'. They did not, however, seek further expansion beyond the recovery of the 'lost territories' of Taiwan, Macao and Hong Kong.[1] The country's new rulers sought to preserve fully the nation's sovereignty and autonomy. They aimed at economic self-sufficiency and were anxious to play an independent, non-aligned, role in world affairs.

The inward-looking and chauvinistic isolationism of the CPC regime has, however, been periodically tempered as a result of ideological, practical and economic considerations.

The nation's commitment to communism and its identification with the oppressed peoples of the Third World has, on occasions, persuaded it to support revolutionary struggles and liberation movements in Africa and Asia and to propagate the 'Chinese model' as the correct communist path to be followed. Such proselytisation has been most evident at times of radicalism at home, for example, during the early stages of the 'Great Leap Forward' and the 'Cultural Revolution'. The amount of economic and military aid sent abroad has, however, remained limited by Soviet standards and China has studiously avoided creating dependency and 'clientship' relationships in these regions.

China's communist rulers have also been acutely aware of the practical realities of the balance of global power between the Soviet and American blocs. They have, on occasions, decided for security reasons to seek temporary accommodations with one of these global camps, first with the Soviet Union during the 1950s, then with America during the 1980s. China has thus played a pivotal role within what has become known as the 'Great Power Triangle'.

Changes in foreign policy have, finally, also been influenced by economic imperatives at home. The need for economic and technical aid persuaded China to seek close ties with the Soviet Union during the 1950s. The need for Western investment and technology to develop the nation's mineral resources and to modernise its factories encouraged the country to adopt a more outward-looking policy during the 1970s and 1980s and to foster closer relations with the United States.

The varied shifts in China's foreign policy direction between 1949 and 1976 are briefly examined in the next section, before attention is

---

[1] The pacific nature of the CPC regime is attested to by the fact that defence spending accounts for only 6-8% of GNP, compared to, for example, the Soviet Union's 12-14%, and that those funds are concentrated upon defensive equipment.

focused on developments since the deaths of Mao Zedong and Zhou Enlai.

Phases in China's Foreign Policy: 1949-1976

'Leaning to One Side' (The Sino-Soviet Alliance): 1949-1962

Maoist China emerged from the 1945-9 revolutionary struggle a diplomatically isolated and economically debilitated nation. Chiang Kai-shek, who had fled to Taiwan, continued to claim rule over mainland China and received America's sympathy. The United States continued to back his Guomindang regime, pledging to ensure Taiwan's security, and refusing to recognise the newly created People's Republic (PRC). Their example was followed by many other Western nations.[1] Under the leadership of President Harry S Truman and Secretary of State John Foster Dulles, America was to remain implacably hostile to the PRC throughout the 1950s, clashing with Chinese troops in Korea in 1950 and blocking its entry into the United Nations, (China's seat remaining occupied by Taiwan).

In such circumstances, and despite policy differences between Stalin and Mao between 1935 and 1949, it was natural that China would turn to the Soviet Union for moral, military and material support as it set about economic reconstruction during the early 1950s. A Treaty of Friendship, Alliance and Mutual Assistance was signed between the two powers in February 1950, establishing a united communist front against capitalism and imperialism. This process of Sino-Soviet rapprochement was described by Mao Zedong as one of 'leaning to one side' and gained China considerable economic benefits. Loans totalling $430 million were provided in 1950 and 1953, in addition to 10 000 technical experts, while new military equipment was sent to a PLA which began to remodel itself on professional Soviet Red Army lines. In the meantime, Russia's nuclear umbrella gave the People's Republic a measure of additional protection against any possible invasion from the still hostile United States.

Despite such close links with the Soviet Union, China did, on occasion, strike out on a line independent of Moscow during the early and mid 1950s. The most notable example of this took place at the Bandung Conference of Asian and African States in Indonesia in April 1955, when the PRC's foreign minister, Zhou Enlai, pledged

[1] Holland, Switzerland, Britain and Scandinavia were exceptions, recognising the PRC during the early 1950s.

China's adherence to the principles of non-aggression and peaceful coexistence and called for a united Afro-Asian front against Western imperialism. This move was the precursor of later Chinese attempts to set itself up as the supporter and leader of a 'third world' of underdeveloped and small to medium nations in a radical non-aligned group, separate from the two superpowers.

China's relations with the Soviet Union, although guarded, remained close until the mid 1950s. They began to cool once Nikita Khrushchev assumed control as the Soviet Union's new leader.[1] The abrasive and impetuous Khrushchev rapidly set about remodelling Russia's domestic and foreign policies. He introduced a series of decentralising economic reforms and denounced Stalin for policy mistakes and political excesses at the Soviet Communist Party's 20th Congress in Moscow in February 1956. In the diplomatic sphere, he called for a new and more conciliatory policy of 'peaceful coexistence'. These policy shifts took place at a time when China itself was making radical adjustments of its own, launching at home the 'Great Leap Forward' which gave new emphasis to the agricultural sector and created the novel commune system, and emerging abroad as a vocal and strident supporter of the new revolutionary movements in Africa and Asia.

Mao Zedong, as a result of his experiences within the CPC during the 1920s, had always been only a lukewarm supporter of the Sino-Soviet pact and had long feared Soviet hegemony. These fears increased during the late 1950s as Russia launched its first space satellite, expanded its nuclear arsenal (developing the world's first Intercontinental Ballistic Missile — ICBM), and attempted to assert control over Chinese forces through the creation of a new 'joint military command'. Mao also took exception to Soviet attempts to assume leadership of the communist bloc and to interpret communist theory as it chose. His distaste for Soviet blustering and arrogance was shared by key colleagues including Zhou Enlai, although Zhou and other moderates, including Peng Dehuai and Liu Shaoqi, saw merits in continuing the alliance.

What made the breach certain, however, was the fact that the antipathy was mutual. Moscow viewed China's new post-1957 domestic policies as 'revisionist' and its foreign policy stance as dangerously aggressive. Thus, step-by-step, the two great communist powers moved from reluctant amity into downright

[1] Khrushchev was elected 1st Secretary of the CPSU following Stalin's death in 1953 and proceeded to concentrate power in his own hands, ousting his rivals Malenkov, Molotov and Bulganin between 1954 and 1958.

hostility between 1958 and 1963. The first clear indication of this rift emerged in August 1959 when the Soviet Union remained firmly neutral during the brief Sino-Indian border war. Moscow subsequently refused to supply China with a sample atomic bomb, and then, in August 1960, it withdrew all its technical personnel from the People's Republic. In 1962 the split was made irrevocable by the Soviet Union's decision to supply fighter aircraft to India, its new Asian ally, during the second Sino-Indian border conflict.

China Searches for a World Role: 1963-1968

During the years immediately following the Sino-Soviet split China sought to establish a new role for itself as leader of the non-aligned Third World and as the true voice of communism. With these objectives in mind, Premier Zhou Enlai made two gruelling tours of Africa and Asia in 1963/4 and 1965 in an attempt to organise a 'second Bandung' to be held in Algeria in 1965. He visited Eastern Europe in 1966. Unfortunately, the Sino-Indian border wars of 1959 and 1962 forfeited China considerable support among Third World nations who greatly respected the Indian prime minister Jawaharlal Nehru. A second Afro-Asian summit failed to materialise, while amongst communist nations only the heretic, Albania, decided to align itself with China in opposition to the Soviet Union.

China's acquisition of its own nuclear capability in October 1964 and the onset of the 'Cultural Revolution' in 1965/6 led to a new bellicosity in the country's approach to foreign affairs. Mao Zedong and his deputy, the PLA leader Lin Biao, began to promote the idea of world revolution through a series of guerrilla wars in the Third World periphery which would result in the encirclement of the 'cities of the world', the United States and Western Europe, and the gradual overthrow of world capitalism. Such talk was pure bravado and was not translated into practical support for Third World revolutionary movements. Instead, as the 'Cultural Revolution' proceeded, China receded into an introspective shell, with foreign affairs falling into abeyance and the diplomatic system being torn apart by factional struggles at home.

China Moves Towards the West:1969-1976

As China slowly emerged out of the chaos of the 'Cultural Revolution' it became clear that major changes were imminent in the 'Great Power Triangle' and China's relations with the Soviet Union continued to deteriorate. Ideologically, the two communist powers had shifted further apart as a result of the 'Cultural Revolution', with its implied criticisms of the Soviet model. On a personal level, the fact that many of Mao's opponents during this internal struggle, including Liu Shaoqi and later Lin Biao, had emerged as Soviet sympathisers exacerbated the rift. Three additional factors further soured relations between the two countries: the Soviet Union's invasion of Czechoslovakia in August 1968 to put down Dubcek's reform movement, which was viewed in China as further evidence of the 'social imperialist' nature of the Soviet regime; the outbreak of border clashes with Russia on the Ussuri river and in Xinjiang in March and June 1969; and the growing influence of the Soviet Union in neighbouring Vietnam.

By 1969, with it clear that the United States had become bogged down in Vietnam and was seeking a means of withdrawal, China's foreign policy theorists, Mao Zedong and Zhou Enlai, began to talk of a realignment in world affairs. It was now the Soviet Union, following the recent increase in Soviet military strength on China's north-eastern border to a total of 40 divisions and its installation of a new contingent of ICBMs, which was seen as the principal threat to the country's security. Rapprochement with the West now seemed sensible for both military and economic reasons. It would enforce greater caution on Soviet activities in South-east Asia, and at the same time give China access to modern Western technology, which would be useful in its new modernisation drive. For the Americans also, there were strong strategic arguments in favour of accommodation with the People's Republic. The US President was finding it increasingly difficult to persuade Congress to vote additional allocations to the military budget as a result of the growth of the peace movement at home. It therefore made sense to reconcile the country's differences with China in an effort to divide Soviet attention and gain a vital breathing-space in the East-West struggle.

With such ends in mind, secret ice-breaking talks began between Zhou Enlai and the American Secretary of State, Henry Kissinger, in July 1971 in Peking. Differences over Taiwan still remained but it was agreed to put this issue on one side in the interests of more pressing, shared, short-term geopolitical goals. Further talks took place three months later and established cordial relations between the leadership of the two countries, with the mandarinates, Kissinger and Zhou Enlai, becoming particularly close friends. The trust and understanding which was generated bore immediate fruit for the People's Republic. China was finally admitted into the

United Nations, at Taiwan's expense, in October 1971, and President Richard Nixon subsequently visited the PRC in February 1972 and signed the Shanghai Communiqué. The communiqué bound both countries to work towards a full normalisation of Sino-American relations and endorsed the principles of 'peaceful coexistence'. It went on to reject the notion of 'spheres of interest' and called for the avoidance of hegemony by any one nation (clearly intended to mean the USSR) in the Asia-Pacific region.

In the short term, these Sino-American agreements failed to prevent the Soviet-backed North Vietnamese forces overrunning South Vietnam in 1975.[1] In the medium term, though, China felt more secure in the knowledge that American forces in the Asian region would no longer be hostile. Rapprochement with the United States served also to accelerate China's rehabilitation into the world community. Chinese diplomatic contacts with the West burgeoned, with Western nations, including Canada, Italy and Spain now extending full recognition, while trade with Europe and America spiralled (see Table 10 on page 83).[2]

The thaw in Sino-American relations did not, however, mean that China had abandoned its desire to develop a new role for itself as a the leader of a radical and non-aligned Third World. Reconciliation with the 'imperialist devil' America was only a tactical and temporary move. China's true vision of foreign affairs was delivered in a speech by Deng Xiaoping to a Special Session of the UN General Assembly in April 1974 when, drawing upon many of Mao's own ideas, he expounded the 'theory of the three worlds'.

Deng, surveying the contemporary world scene, declared that the traditional Leninist division of the globe into two contending camps, socialist and imperialist, was no longer valid. The Soviet Union, through its actions in Eastern Europe, South-east Asia and Africa, had transformed itself into a second imperialist power, vying now for global hegemony with the United States. These two superpowers occupied what was termed the 'first world' in the new Chinese analysis. In the 'second world' stood the developed countries of Europe, while the 'third world' comprised the developing nations of Asia (including China), Africa and Latin America (AALA). China believed that both of the latter groupings

[1] US troops withdrew from Saigon in 1975.

[2] Henry Kissinger paid further visits to Peking in 1973, 1974 and in December 1975, being accompanied on the last occasion by Gerald Ford, who had assumed the American presidency following the Watergate crisis of 1973-4. Liaison offices were opened in Washington and Peking in May 1973.

were anxious to avoid the hegemony of either of the 'first world' superpowers. China thus sought to promote greater unity among the European nations and to encourage 'second world' nations to strengthen their resistance to the Soviet military threat and reduce their dependence on the American strategic umbrella. It sought, also, to foster a spirit of co-operation, independence and self-reliance among the 'third world' countries, with the ultimate aim of creating a new world economic order which would be based on the principles of equality and mutual benefit. It saw the emergence of the OPEC oil cartel in the wake of the October 1973 Arab-Israeli war as one hopeful step in this direction.

In pursuance of this 'three worlds' policy, the Chinese leadership made strenuous efforts to improve contacts with Europe and AALA countries. In May 1975 Deputy Premier Deng Xiaoping paid a state visit to France, the first ever to a Western country by a senior Chinese leader, when he extended his country's official recognition of the EEC. The prime ministers of Britain, West Germany and Belgium also visited China in the same year. Meanwhile, among the nations of the Third World, Brazil, Grenada, the Gambia and Niger established diplomatic relations with China for the first time. This new 'three worlds' policy was one of a united front, regardless of political ideology, between the nations of the 'second' and 'third' worlds.[1] Conservative leaders, for example Franz-Josef Strauss of West Germany, Georges Pompidou of France and Edward Heath of Britain, were greeted as warmly in China as leaders of socialist parties, while in the neighbouring Asia-Pacific region, the dictatorships of the Philippines and Thailand were cultivated in an effort to strengthen resistance to the Soviet-Vietnamese threat.[2]

Foreign Policy After the Fall of Mao and Zhou

During the years between 1949 and 1976 Mao Zedong and Zhou Enlai had been the two dominant influences on China's foreign policy. Day-to-day operations had been controlled by the sophisticated diplomat Zhou Enlai, who had continued to attend conferences and embark on overseas tours even after he had

[1] This heretical stance led to a rift in relations between China and a number of former communist allies, including Albania, but to an improvement in relations with, for example, Tito's non-aligned Yugoslavia.

[2] Diplomatic relations were opened with the ASEAN nations of Malaysia, Thailand and the Philippines in 1974 and 1975.

officially relinquished the post of foreign minister in 1958.[1] Zhou also had a major input into China's foreign policy formulation, taking, for example, a leading role in the Bandung non-aligned strategy and being an early supporter of *détente* with the United States. Mao Zedong, by contrast, had devoted most of his time to domestic and party affairs and, although he frequently met foreign dignitaries in Peking, he only twice ventured abroad himself (on both occasions visiting Moscow). It had, however, been Mao Zedong who had instigated most of the major shifts in the Chinese foreign policy, including the break from Moscow and the 'Three Worlds Theory'.

However, although these two figures had been the controlling influences over China's foreign policy, significant consensus had existed within the CPC élite between 1949 and 1976. This meant that the deaths of Zhou and Mao in 1976 did not lead to a major reorientation in China's policy stance. Instead, their successors, Hua Guofeng, Deng Xiaoping and foreign minister Huang Hua, slowly built upon past achievements.

From Tokyo to Lang Son: 1977-1979

China's policy of rapprochement with the West and with capitalist neighbours in the Pacific region gained pace after 1977, as investment capital and modern industrial and military technology were sought to make possible Hua and Deng's ambitious modernisation programmes.

Particular progress was made in relations with Japan, China's traditional enemy and rival. Sino-Japanese relations began to soften during the 1970s. Diplomatic contacts increased and commercial relations developed to such an extent that by 1975 Japan had emerged as China's principal trading partner. It imported raw materials, exporting in return capital goods, in what became a mutually beneficial and complementary relationship. These improved relations were underlined in 1978 by the signing of a $10 billion bilateral barter trade agreement (exchanging Chinese oil and coal for Japanese steel and advanced technology equipment) and a new Treaty of Peace and Friendship.

Of even greater significance was the full normalisation of relations with the United States which was achieved in December

[1] Chen Yi succeeded Zhou Enlai as Foreign Minister in 1958. Ji Pengfei temporarily took over from Chen after his death in 1972, before the Maoist Qiao Guanhua assumed office.

1978 after America's new President, Jimmy Carter, made a number of significant concessions. The United States now agreed to recognise the People's Republic as the sole legal government of China. It terminated its official diplomatic relations with Taiwan; it rescinded the American-Taiwanese mutual defence treaty; and it agreed to withdraw its troops from Taiwan. China, in return, agreed reluctantly to tolerate continuing American economic contacts with Taiwan and the sale of a limited number of defensive weapons. This agreement, which represented the culmination of almost a decade of careful diplomacy between the two nations, finally removed any lingering American threat to the Chinese mainland. It was succeeded by a warmly received inaugural visit to Washington by Deng Xiaoping in January 1979. Two months later, embassies were established in Washington and Peking and later in the same year a Sino-American commercial treaty was concluded granting China 'most favoured nation' status.

During this period of rapprochement with the West, relations with the Soviet Union continued to deteriorate. China was particularly alarmed by Soviet advances in Africa and the Middle East where it installed proxy regimes in Angola, Mozambique, Ethiopia, South Yemen and Afghanistan between 1974 and 1979, and by the actions of the Soviet Union's South-east Asian partner, Vietnam.

Vietnam, once a close ally of China, had, as a result of its exhausting 16-year war of unification (1959-75), become progressively dependent upon the Soviet Union for economic and military aid. By the late 1970s its ties with Moscow were unusually close. It joined Comecon in July 1978 and signed a friendship treaty with the Soviet Union in November of the same year. These developments vexed China's leaders, who saw Vietnam emerging as an 'Asian Cuba' on its southern doorstep. They feared it would attempt to foment revolution and gain control over the entire Indochinese peninsula, thus challenging China's paramountcy in a vital region.

Such fears appeared to be confirmed during 1978. The Vietnamese government began persecuting ethnic Chinese living within its borders, forcing thousands to flee, before launching a major invasion into neighbouring Cambodia in December 1978. Hanoi proceeded to overthrow the brutal, but Chinese-backed, Pol Pot (Khmer Rouge) regime and installed in power in January 1979 a puppet government, the Kampuchean National United Front, led by Heng Samrin. Faced with such blatant expansionism, the

Chinese government, with Vice-Premier Deng Xiaoping taking the lead, decided in 1979 that the time had arrived for it to teach its southern cousin a salutary lesson. It sought, following the example set during the 1962 Sino-Indian border war, to inflict a humbling military defeat on an army which claimed to be the 'third strongest in the world' through a brief thrust into Vietnam.[1]

This border offensive was launched on 17 February 1979, when 150 000 Chinese troops crossed into North Vietnam with orders to advance for 30 miles, capture provincial capitals, defeat the main Vietnamese forces and then return home. The venture proved, however, to be an embarrassment for the PLA. The Chinese forces did take control of the important provincial town of Lang Son on 2 March but failed to engage Vietnam's main forces, which were in Cambodia. The PLA suffered the loss of 26 000 men and serious injuries to a further 37 000 following skirmishes with the enemy's small, but well equipped, border units. The PLA withdrew into China on 16 March, claiming to have achieved its aims. In reality, however, neither side emerged victorious. Vietnam had inflicted significant casualties on PLA forces and remained in firm control of Cambodia, but had shown caution and timidity by avoiding full-scale conflict with its northern neighbour. China could thus claim to have made clear to Vietnam that any future expansion would encounter its resistance and bear a heavy price. In addition, China had succeeded in bringing the Cambodian issue to the world's attention and to swing world opinion against Hanoi. This became clear in 1980, when the UN voted to continue to recognise the Pol Pot regime as the legitimate government of Cambodia and called upon Vietnam to withdraw its troops.

The Door Stays Open to the West: 1980-1984

China's contacts with the West continued to broaden and deepen during the years after 1980 as its modernisation programme gained pace. China was now accepted into a wide range of international organisations, including the World Bank. Its leaders, Deng Xiaoping, Zhao Ziyang, Hu Yaobang, Huang Hua and Li Xiannian,[2] made frequent

[1]   China cut off all remaining economic aid to Vietnam in July 1978.

[2]   Hua Guofeng, who had been active in Chinese diplomacy between 1976-80, receded from view in 1981 following his displacement as CPC Chairman. Huang Hua was replaced as Foreign Minister by Wu Xueqian, a former YCL colleague of Hu Yaobang, in November 1982.

trips abroad and met foreign dignitaries in Peking. Its citizens engaged in cultural and sporting exchanges, and substantial trade links were established with nations throughout the world. A notable feature of this period was the casting aside of old political and ideological differences by the new Deng administration as relations with ASEAN powers and even India significantly improved. The one exception continued to be the Soviet Union, with whom relations continued to deteriorate as a result of Russia's zealous expansionism.

Sino-Soviet relations plunged to a new low when Russian troops moved into Afghanistan on 26 December 1979, deposed and executed its troubled Marxist ruler, Hafizullah Amin, and installed a puppet administration under the leadership of Babrak Karmal. This action was viewed through Chinese eyes as part of a longer-term Soviet 'southward drive' towards the Indian and Pacific Oceans, aimed at outflanking both Western Europe and China. It gave strength to China's calls for a united front against the shared Soviet threat and served to strengthen Sino-European and Sino-American relations. China was therefore heartened in 1980 to see Europe and America taking more strenuous economic and military actions to isolate Russia and to see Soviet-American *détente* finally collapse. Major increases took place in Western defence spending in the aftermath of Afghanistan and continued to take place in 1981 as a result of Western distaste for the Soviet-backed repression of the 'Solidarity' free trade union movement in Poland.

Afghanistan and Poland proved, in retrospect, to be turning-points for Soviet expansionism. By the end of 1981 Russia had more than 100 000 troops tied up in Afghanistan by the Islamic *mujahadeen* guerrillas, who retained control over the rural hinterland. In Europe, the Soviet Union was faced by a stronger and more determined NATO, which was in the process of installing a new type of intermediate-range nuclear weapon. In America, it was confronted by a belligerent, new Republican administration under the leadership of Ronald Reagan which was rearming at an unprecedented pace, modernising its navy and nuclear arsenal and establishing a new 220 000 Rapid Deployment Force in the Gulf region.

These developments, taken together with Soviet economic and political difficulties at home, significantly altered the balance of world power and served to diminish the threat posed to China from the north. This power shift was recognised, with typical prescience, by Deng Xiaoping in early 1981 when he speculated that the Soviet Union was entering a period of secular decline.

This weakening of Soviet paramountcy served to make the American connection less vital for Chinese policy-makers and it was noticeable that Sino-American relations began to cool from 1981. One important factor behind this deterioration in relations was the entry into the White House in January 1981 of President Reagan. Reagan, a committed anti-communist and a supporter of the Taiwanese cause, had promised during his 1980 election campaign to supply sophisticated new weapons and extend diplomatic recognition to Taiwan, in what was known as a new 'Two Chinas Policy'. Such a policy was totally unacceptable to the Chinese, who, while willing to tolerate US economic contacts with Taiwan and small sales of defensive armaments, drew the line at official recognition and the supply of sophisticated military technology. If implemented, this policy would have led to a complete breach in Sino-Soviet relations. This was recognised by the American State Department, headed by Alexander Haig, who managed to persuade President Reagan, after assuming office, to drop the idea of the recognition of Taiwan in the broader interests of sustaining the joint Sino-American strategic front against the Soviet Union. However, while this succeeded in preventing a rupture, Sino-American relations remained guarded and wary in the years after 1981, with the issue of US arms sales to Taiwan continuing to disturb Peking.

The emerging differences between China and the United States persuaded the Soviet Union during this period to attempt to woo back its former communist ally and heal the 20-year Sino-Soviet rift. Moscow's new diplomatic offensive was launched by the CPSU's leader, Leonid Brezhnev, who travelled to Tashkent near the Chinese border to appeal for a normalisation in relations in a significant speech in March 1982. Five months later, Chinese representatives visited Moscow to renew contacts with the Soviet Union and a series of middle-level talks began between the two nations in Peking in October 1982. These discussions gained added impetus in 1983, after Yuri Andropov had replaced Brezhnev (who had died in November 1982) as the CPSU leader.

There was thus a modest thaw in Sino-Soviet relations in the years after 1982, with commercial contacts in particular increasing. However, China continued to regard the Soviet Union as its principal enemy and four significant obstacles still remained in the path of a full reconciliation: lingering differences over border demarcations; the presence of Soviet troops and SS-20 missiles in the Far East; continued Russian occupation of Afghanistan; and Moscow's support for Vietnam and its Cambodian satellite.

Relations between China and Vietnam also remained hostile during the period between 1980 and 1984, with border clashes being frequent and often serious. Vietnam continued to provide sustenance to the Heng Semrin regime in Cambodia through the presence of 200 000 of its own troops, while China continued to organise resistance through diplomatic and military channels. It persuaded Third World countries in the United Nations to maintain recognition of the deposed Pol Pot government and prompted the neighbouring countries of ASEAN (Thailand, Singapore, Malaysia, the Philippines and Indonesia) to assist Cambodia's guerrillas through the establishment of a broad-based, united resistance front, comprising the Khmer Rouge, in addition to the Cambodian nationalist leaders Prince Sihanouk (Cambodia's head of state prior to 1970) and Sonn Sann (the country's former prime minister).

However, while the need for increased economic contacts with the West and continued resistance to the Soviet-Vietnamese threat remained the two guiding principles in China's foreign policy between 1980 and 1984, a third, and more novel, policy objective also began to emerge. This was the CPC leadership's desire to achieve national reunification and to recover the lost sovereignty of Taiwan, Macao and Hong Kong. Increased priority was given to this longstanding aspiration and significant advances were made towards achieving these goals during the years after 1980.

Early impetus was given to the reunification process by the December 1978 Sino-American 'normalisation agreement', following which the United States severed its diplomatic ties with Taiwan. This removed one significant obstacle and persuaded the Deng administration to devise an attractive new framework for unification – the 'one country, two systems' strategy. This envisaged the 'lost territories' of Taiwan (population 19 million), Hong Kong (a British Crown Colony with a population of 6 million) and Macao (a Portuguese possession granted quasi-independence in 1976 with a population of 0.3 million) being allowed to retain their existing capitalist economic and social structures and considerable political autonomy, but transferring territorial sovereignty to the People's Republic. They would become 'Special Administrative Regions' (SARs), with powers to raise their own taxes, control revenue expenditure and elect their local legislatures; but China would retain ultimate control over their defence and oversee each region's affairs through a Chief Executive appointed following mutual consultation. The new SARs would continue to function, in addition, as free-trading areas, giving China continued access to foreign markets and foreign exchange.

To make this new policy work China had to convince the citizens and leaders of its 'lost territories' that it would genuinely and longstandingly tolerate such dualism in economic and social affairs. A series of confidence-building initiatives were thus launched. These included the SEZ programme (see page 83), the NPC's codification of new commercial laws and the encouragement of overseas Chinese to participate to a greater degree in their homeland's modernisation through investing in mainland industries and attending meetings of the CPPCC. The Chinese government also adopted a more conciliatory tone towards the political leadership of the 'lost territories', stressing its desire for peaceful reunification rather than 'liberation' by force.

However, despite such moderation, the mainland's overtures continued to be rejected by the leadership of the largest, and most significant, of the 'lost territories', Taiwan.[1] This island had been ruled since 1949 by the Guomindang, first under Chiang Kai-shek and then, following his death in 1975, by his elderly son Chiang Ching-kuo. The Guomindang was predominantly staffed by ageing former mainlanders who formed only a 15% minority on the island and who continued to claim to be the legitimate rulers of all China. They were unpopular with the ethnic Taiwanese majority community and had to rule through force and repression. However, both the Guomindang and the islanders were united on one point, their antipathy towards communism and their refusal to countenance any transfer of sovereignty to Peking. They concentrated their joint efforts, in the years between 1949 and 1980, upon establishing a viable and thriving economy and a powerful and sophisticated military force. With initial US aid they succeeded in this, and they were able, between 1980-84, to stand alone and reject outside pressures to make a deal with mainland China.

Hong Kong, by contrast, was less able, for both commercial and political reasons, to reject China's new reunification overtures. The bulk of its territory was connected directly to China by land and was heavily dependent upon the mainland for food, raw materials and fuel. Consequently, commercial links between Hong Kong and

[1] China had even offered Taiwan the additional concession of continued control over the island's military and police forces once sovereignty had been transferred to Peking.

China were unusually close. In 1984, for example, China accounted for a third of all foreign investment in Hong Kong and took 8% of the Crown Colony's exports and 34% of its re-exports. Hong Kong, in return, provided a market for 25% of China's exports and functioned as an *entrepôt* middleman between the mainland and Western world, furnishing China with a third of its foreign exchange requirements. Politically, only a tenth of the Hong Kong territories (Hong Kong island and neighbouring Kowloon Peninsula) had been granted in perpetuity to Britain in the 'unequal' and disputed treaties of 1842 and 1860. The remainder was held on a 99-year lease, which was due to expire in 1997. The colony, without these leased lands, was indefensible and unviable. This made the British government, anxious to remain on cordial terms with the new Chinese government for commercial reasons, willing to commence negotiations with Peking in 1979.

China maintained a firm posture on the question of sovereignty during these early discussions. It stressed, however, its willingness to allow the existing economic system to remain in place after 1997 and encouraged Hong Kong businessmen to participate in its SEZ ventures, an opportunity which was grasped eagerly by a community anxious to foster good relations with Peking. Top-level talks recommenced in 1982. Britain, at first, appeared unwilling to transfer sovereignty in 1997 but was eventually persuaded by the practical realities of the situation and assented to a compromise agreement signed in December 1984. Under the terms of this accord, the 'Joint Declaration of the Governments of the United Kingdom and the People's Republic on the Question of Hong Kong', Britain acceded to the full transfer of sovereignty in 1997, while China agreed in return to grant Hong Kong SAR status and pledged to guarantee that its existing economic and social system, including the freedoms of speech, press and association, would be allowed to remain unchanged for a period of 50 years after transfer.[1]

These represented the most favourable terms which the British government could have anticipated and included a number of significant concessions by Peking. However, Hong Kong's residents, remembering mainland ·China's turbulent recent history, remained understandably apprehensive about the future after 1997. They feared a lurch back towards leftist extremism in Peking, which would, at some future date, lead to the termination

---

[1] The Hong Kong SAR would be allowed in the future to make its own economic and cultural agreements with foreign states and join the GATT.

of their privileged economic and political status and fatally damage the prosperity of their successful capitalist enclave.

Foreign Policy after 1984: A Thaw in Sino-Soviet Relations?

President Reagan visited China for the first time in May 1984 in an attempt both to boost his image at home during a re-election year and to mend fences with an increasingly wary Deng administration. He was largely successful in his latter aim, making a series of concessions to China on economic and military matters. The United States reduced its restrictions on high-technology exports to China, relaxed its textile import quota and pledged, once again, to work towards a gradual reduction in its arms sales to Taiwan. However, it became clear during 1985 and 1986 that China's relationship with the United States would never fully return to the intimacy of 1978-81. China was seeking instead to strike out on a determinedly independent line between the two superpowers. It felt, following the successful tests of its own land- and sea-based ICBMs in 1980 and 1982 and the modernisation of the PLA, more confident of its own defensive capabilities, and it feared that the United States had become too powerful and dominant a force on the world stage.

China thus attempted in the years after 1984, firstly to re-establish itself as the leader of the non-aligned Third World. Zhao Ziyang, Hu Yaobang, Wu Xueqian and Li Xiannian embarked upon tours of Africa, Asia and Latin America and renewed their calls for the establishment of more just world economic order. There appeared to be, also, a greater willingness to improve relations with the Soviet Union and bring to an end two decades of mutual hostility. Significant differences still existed between the two communist nations on questions of ideology and over the issues of border security, Afghanistan and Cambodia, but solutions to these problems appeared to be slowly emerging in 1985 and 1986.

The coming to power of the Gorbachev administration in the Soviet Union in March 1985 was a particularly hopeful development for Peking. The new administration placed prime emphasis on reviving the Soviet economy and introduced a number of reforms which borrowed elements from the post-1978 Deng programme. This served somewhat to narrow the ideological divide between the two nations. The Gorbachev administration sought also to divert military resources from its southern and eastern borders and appeared anxious to find solutions to the problems of Afghanistan and Cambodia.

In Afghanistan the Soviet government became willing to countenance troop withdrawal on condition that a régime sympathetic to Moscow was allowed to retain control following its departure. It began to make moves towards fostering a new 'broad front' coalition form of government, which would include tribal and religious chiefs. It allowed non-communist politicians to contest elections and participate in the government in 1985 and, in May 1986, helped to engineer the replacement of the leader of the 1979 coup, Babrak Karmal, by the more conciliatory figure of Dr Najibullah Ahmadzai, a Pathan who had formerly headed the KGB-trained Afghan secret police. These actions were followed in October 1986 by the withdrawal of 8 000 of the 115 000 Soviet troops in Afghanistan and in January 1987 by the imposition of a six-month unilateral Soviet ceasefire while UN-sponsored peace negotiations continued in Geneva.

In Cambodia, where 170 000 Vietnamese troops remained firmly entrenched despite continuing guerrilla assaults, China took the lead in the search for a compromise solution. It persuaded the reviled Pol Pot to step down as the Khmer Rouge leader in September 1985 in a gesture aimed at expediting an early withdrawal of Hanoi's forces.[1] However, border skirmishes continued along the Vietnam-China border, reaching serious proportions in October 1986 and January 1987 when an estimated 700 Chinese and 300 Vietnamese troops were killed during cross-border raids.

The move towards Sino-Soviet rapprochement was given additional impetus by the concessions offered on border questions by Mikhail Gorbachev in a major 'olive-branch' speech delivered at Vladivostok in the Soviet Far-East in July 1986. The Soviet leader gave considerable ground over the disputed demarcation of the Amur and Ussuri river borders in north-eastern China and promised to reduce substantially the numbers of Soviet troops (then totalling 450 000) stationed on its 'Eastern Front', commencing with the pull-out of 11 000 soldiers from Soviet-backed Outer Mongolia during the spring of 1987.

Such conciliatory moves resulted in a marked thawing in relations between the two great communist powers and appeared

---

[1] Vietnam has separately stated its determination to withdraw from Cambodia in 1990, believing that the Heng Samrin government would, by then, be powerful enough to survive on its own.

to leave the door open to a full normalisation of Sino-Soviet relations in the near future. In the meantime, however, commercial and diplomatic contacts between China and the Soviet Union increased significantly, with a $14 billion five-year trade pact being signed by Vice-Premier Yao Yilin in Moscow in July 1985. This involved the exchange of Soviet machine goods for Chinese consumer goods and agricultural produce, increased Russian co-operation in China's economic modernisation programme and the envisaged doubling of two-way commerce by 1990. Also, a consular agreement was signed between the two nations in September 1986. Party relations have also improved, with China now referring to the Soviet leader as 'Comrade' Gorbachev. Such an improvement in relations is to be expected when the Deng faction's sympathy for the Soviet Union during the 1950s and 1960s is remembered. Sino-Soviet relations will never, however, fully return to the intimacy of the 1950s. China continues to reject the Soviet Union's claims to leadership of the world communist movement and dislikes the attitude of superiority it still displays towards its poorer Asian brother. Dengist China seeks rather to be treated on equal terms and to steer an autonomous course between the two superpowers.

The Deng administration's concern to achieve the rapid reunification of China's 'lost territories' has remained unabated in the period since 1984. In Hong Kong, further progress has been made in preparation for the 1997 transfer of sovereignty. A Sino-British Joint Liaison Group has now been established and a 59-member Drafting Committee (23 of whose members have been drawn from Hong Kong) has begun work on the drafting of a constitution ('Basic Law') for the SAR which will be submitted to the NPC in 1990. The British authorities have also begun transferring power to a new Legislative Council in an effort to give the colony's citizens experience of administration prior to 1997. China has, however, displayed concern at the zeal with which Britain has been devolving power to the Hong Kong people and has objected to the introduction of democratic local electoral systems which run at stark variance with the Peking model.

China's other lost coastal enclave, Macao, which had been under Portuguese *de facto* control since 1557 and *de jure* control since 1887 (when China's Imperial government recognised Portugal's sovereign rights to the port), has similarly been renegotiated back to China under a Hong Kong style 'one country, two systems' agreement. Negotiations with the Portuguese government had been going on since 1979, when full diplomatic relations between Portugal and the PRC were established for the first time. These talks gained momentum after the May 1985 visit of President Eanes to Peking and culminated in the signing of the 'Macao treaty' of April 1987 in which Portugal agreed to hand over sovereignty on 20 December 1999 and China assented in return to allow Macao's capitalist system, which is based around a combination of gambling casinos, nightclubs and tourist hotels, to remain in place for at least 50 years.

Unlike the progress made with Hong Kong and Macao, little progress has been made in persuading Taiwan, the largest and most significant of China's 'lost territories', to consider a 'Hong Kong-Macao solution'. The Taipei government remains intransigent in its refusal to countenance official contact with Peking and appears likely to adhere to this stance throughout the rest of this and the next decade. But problems will mount for Taiwan in the more distant future. The diminishing supply of arms from the United States coupled with the loss of Hong Kong as an acceptable conduit for trade with China after 1997 will cause serious economic and military difficulties, at a time when the leadership of the island will pass into the hands of a new generation of ethnic Taiwanese. These leaders will be tempted to declare full independence from China, creating a serious dilemma for the CPC in Peking.

APPENDIX A: THE ADMINISTRATIVE DIVISIONS OF CHINA

The PRC on its establishment in October 1949 was originally divided into six Great Administrative Areas – the North, North-east, North-west, South-west, East and Central-South – which were governed by joint military-civilian CPC commands. The Great Administrative Areas were abolished in June 1954 as a result of Peking's concern with the growing independent-mindedness of a number of regional governors, most notably Gao Gang in the North-east and Rao Shushi in the East, and the centre began to deal directly with the provincial rung of administration below. The 1949-54 regions have survived as entities for economic planning. Today, however, it is the 21 provinces (*sheng*), which boast populations varying from 4 million to 101 million apiece (see Table A1), which constitute the uppermost tier of local government in the PRC. Below the provinces are 210 prefectures (*diqu*), in which special appointed administrative agencies function, 2138 counties (*xian*), 190 cities (*shi*: see Table A2), and, at the bottom rung of the organisational hierarchy, thousands of small townships and administrative villages (*xiang*). Five special provincial-level Autonomous Regions were progressively established between 1949 and 1965 for regions in which minority nationalities (see Table A3) constituted a substantial proportion of the local population. These Autonomous Regions enjoy little real political autonomy, but are allowed to conduct government business in the language of the region and to uphold local customs and culture. Smaller autonomous areas (*zhou*), prefectures and counties have also been established. Finally, the country's three largest cities, Peking, Shanghai and Tientsin, enjoy special status as municipalities of provincial rank, dealing directly with the central government.

117

TABLE A1: The Provinces, Regions and Municipalities of China

PROVINCES (Pinyin)	Wade-Giles	AREA ('000) (sq km)	POPU- LATION ('000) 1984	CAPITAL (Pinyin)
Anhui	Anhwei	139	51 030	Hefei
Fujian	Fukien	121	26 770	Fuzhou
Gansu	Kansu	454	20 160	Lanzhou
Guangdong	Kwangtung	212	61 660	Guangzhou
Guizhou	Kweichow	176	29 320	Guiyang
Hebei	Hopei	188	54 870	Shijiazhuang
Heilongjiang	Heilungkiang	469	32 950	Harbin
Henan	Honan	167	76 460	Zhengzhou
Hubei	Hupeh	186	48 760	Wuhan
Hunan	Hunan	210	55 610	Changsha
Jiangsu	Kiangsu	103	61 710	Nanjing
Jiangxi	Kiangsi	169	34 210	Nanchang
Jilin	Kirin	187	22 840	Changchun
Liaoning	Liaoning	146	36 550	Shenyang
Qinghai	Tsinghai	721	4020	Xining
Shaanxi	Shensi	206	29 660	Xian
Shanxi	Shansi	156	26 000	Taiyuan
Shandong	Shantung	153	76 370	Jinan
Sichuan	Szechwan	567	101 120	Chengdu
Yunnan	Yunnan	394	33 620	Kunming
Zhejiang	Chekiang	102	39 930	Hangzhou

AUTONOMOUS REGIONS

Guangxi Zhuang	Kwangsi Chuang	236	38 060	Nanning
Nei Monggol	Inner Mongolia	1183	19 850	Hohhot
Ningxia Hui	Ningshia Hui	66	4060	Yinchuan
Xinjiang Uygur	Sinkiang Uighur	1600	13 440	Urumqi
Xizang	Tibet	1228	1970	Lhasa

MUNICIPALITIES

Beijing	Peking	17	9470	—
Shanghai	Shanghai	6	12 050	—
Tianjin	Tientsin	11	7990	—
ALL CHINA		9571	1 030 510	Beijing

TABLE A2: China's Principle Cities[1]

CITY (Pinyin)	Wade-Giles	PROVINCE (Pinyin)	1985 POPU- LATION ('000)
Shanghai	Shang-hai	—	6980
Beijing	Peking	—	5860
Tianjin	Tientsin	—	5380
Shenyang	Shen-yang or Mukden	Liaoning	4200
Wuhan	Wu-han or Hankow	Hubei	3400
Guangzhou	Canton	Guangdong	3290
Chongqing	Chungking	Sichuan	2780
Harbin	Ha-erh-pin	Heilongjiang	2630
Chengdu	Ch'eng-tu	Sichuan	2580
Xian	Hsi-an or Sian	Shaanxi	2330
Zibo	Tzepo	Shandong	2300
Nanjing	Nanking	Jiangsu	2250
Taiyuan	T'ai-yuan	Shanxi	1880
Changchun	Ch'ang-ch'un	Jilin	1860
Dalian	Dairen or Luda	Liaoning	1630
Zaozhuang		Shandong	1590
Zhengzhou	Chengchow	Henan	1590
Kunming	K'un-ming	Yunnan	1490
Tangshan	T'ang-shan	Hebei	1390
Suzhou	Soochow	Jiangsu	1280
Hangzhou	Hangchow	Zhejiang	1250
Changsha	Chang-sha	Hunan	1160
Nanchang	Nan-ch'ang	Jiangxi	1120
Urumqi	Urumchi	Xinjiang Uygur	1000
Datong	Tatung	Shaanxi	1000
Hefei	Hofei	Anhui	850

[1] Included are all cities with a population in excess of 1.5 million as well as other smaller centres which are mentioned in the text. The population totals are those for the centres of the cities and do not include the surrounding suburbs.

TABLE A3: China's Principal Minority Nationalities

NAME OF NATIONALITY	1978 POPU- LATION ('000)	CENTRES OF DISTRIBUTION
Zuang	12 000	Guangxi-Zhuang & South-west
Hui	6400	Ningxia-Hui, Gansu & North-central China
Uygur	5400	Xinjiang-Uygur
Yi	4300	Sichuan & South-west
Miao	3900	South-west
Tibetan	3400	Xizang & South-west
Manchu	2600	North-east & Nei Monggol
Mongol	2600	Nei Monggol & North-east
Bouyei	1700	Guizhou
Korean	1600	North-east
Yao	1200	Guangxi-Zhuang & South-west
Dong	1100	Guizhou & South-west
Bai	1000	Yunnan
Hani	960	Yunnan
Kazakh	800	Xinjiang-Uygur, Gansu & Qinghai
Tujia	770	Hunan & Hubei
Dai	760	Yunnan
Li	680	Guangdong

[1] Included are minority nationalities with populations in excess of 500 000.

APPENDIX B: PARTY CONGRESSES AND NATIONAL PEOPLE'S CONGRESSES

TABLE B1: CPC National Congresses

Congress Number	Location	Date
First	Shanghai	1921 July
Second	Shanghai	1922 July
Third	Canton	1923 June
Fourth	Shanghai	1925 Jan
Fifth	Wuhan	1927 April–May
Sixth	Moscow	1928 June–July
Seventh	Yanan	1945 April–June
Eighth	Peking	1956 Sept
Eighth[1]	Peking	1958 May
Ninth	Peking	1969 April
Tenth	Peking	1973 Aug
Eleventh	Peking	1977 Aug
Twelfth	Peking	1982 Sept

[1] Second Session

National People's Congresses

Congress Number	Location	Date of First Convening	Number of Delegates
First	Peking	1954 Sept	1226
Second	Peking	1959 April	1226
Third	Peking	1964/5 Dec–Jan	3040
Fourth	Peking	1975 Jan	2885
Fifth	Peking	1978 Feb–Mar	3497
Sixth	Peking	1983 June	2978

121

TABLE C1: Key State Institutions

State President: Li Xiannian

Vice-President: Gen. Ulanhu

*THE NATIONAL PEOPLE'S CONGRESS STANDING COMMITTEE
(INNER COUNCIL)*

Chairman Peng Zhen[1]
Vice-Chairmen

Chen Pixian[2]	Bainqen Erdini Qoigyi
Gen. Wei Guoqing	Gyaincain (Panchem Lama)
Peng Chong	Zhu Xuefan
Gen. Seypidin	Wang Renzhong
Geng Biao	Zhou Gucheng
Ngapoi Ngawang Jigme	Yan Jici
Xu Deheng	Lt-Gen. Liao Hansheng
Hu Juewen	Col-Gen. Han Xianchu
Hu Yuzhi	Huang Hua
Rong Yiren	Ye Fei

Secretary-General Wang Hanbin

STATE COUNCIL (SEPTEMBER 1986)

Prime Minister Zhao Ziyang [1]
Vice-Premiers Wan Li,[1,2] Yao Yilin,[1] Li Peng.[1,2] Tian Jiyun,[1,2] Qiao Shi[1,2]
State Councillors

Fang Yi[1]	Ji Pengfei	Gen. Zhang Aiping
Gu Mu	Zhang Jingfu	Song Ping
Kang Shien	Wang Bingqian	Song Jian
Miss Chen Muhua[1]	Wu Xueqian[1]	

Secretary-General Chen Junsheng
Auditor-General Lu Peijian
President of the People's Bank of China Miss Chen Muhua[1]
Minister in Charge of:
State Planning Commission Song Ping
State Economic Commission Lu Dong
State Commission for Restructuring the Economic System Zhao Ziyang[1]
State Education Commission Li Peng[1,2]
State Scientific and Technological Commission Song Jian
Commission of Science, Technology and Industry

for National Defence Ding Henggao
State Nationalities Affairs Commission Ismail Amat
State Physical Culture and Sports Commission Li Menghua
State Family Planning Commission Wang Wei
Ministers of:
Foreign Affairs Wu Xueqian[1]
National Defence Gen. Zhang Aiping
Public Security Ruan Chongwu
State Security Jia Chungwang
Civil Affairs Cui Naifu
Justice Zou Yu
Finance Wang Bingqian
Commerce Liu Yi
Foreign Economic Relations and Trade Zheng Tuobin
Agriculture, Animal Husbandry and Fishery He Kang
Forestry Yang Zhong
Water Conservancy and Electric Power Miss Qian Zhengying
Urban and Rural Construction and Environmental Protection Ye Rutang
Geology and Minerals Zhu Xun
Metallurgical Industry Qi Yuanjing
Machine-Building Industry Vacant
Nuclear Industry Jiang Xinxiong
Aviation Industry Mo Wenxiang
Electronics Industry Li Tieying
Ordnance Industry Zhou Jiahua
Astronautics Industry Li Xue
Coal Industry Yu Hongen
Petroleum Industry Wang Tao
Chemical Industry Qin Zhongda
Textile Industry Miss Wu Wenying
Light Industry Yang Bo
Railways Ding Guangeng
Communications Qian Yongchang
Posts and Telecommunications Yang Taifang
Labour and Personnel Zhao Dongwan
Culture Wang Meng
Radio, Films and Television Ai Zhisheng
Public Health Cui Yueli
PRESIDENT OF THE SUPREME PEOPLE'S COURT Zheng Tianxiang
PROCURATOR-GENERAL Yang Yichen

[1] Members of CPC Politbureau
[2] Members of CPC Secretariat

GLOSSARY

LIST OF ABBREVIATIONS, CHINESE TERMS AND ADDITIONAL BIOGRAPHICAL INFORMATION

AALA Africa, Asian and Latin American nations.

apparatchik Russian term for a member of the party apparatus.

AR Autonomous Region established in areas of minority nationality concentration.

ASEAN Association of South-East-Asian Nations. A regional, political and commercial grouping formed in 1967 of Indonesia, Singapore, Malaysia, the Philippines, Thailand and (since 1984) Brunei.

Boxer Rebellion anti-foreigner uprising in Peking, Shaanxi and Manchuria in 1900 which was encouraged by the Dowager-Empress Ci Xi.

bourgeois liberalism catch-all term referring to destabilising Western cultural and democratic ideas.

CAC Central Advisory Commission. Advisory body of senior and retired party luminaries.

CCID Central Commission for Inspecting Discipline. The CPC's ideological and disciplinary watchdog which is chaired by Chen Yun.

Chen Yun (*Ch'en Yun* 1905-) born in Shanghai, Chen trained as a typesetter and joined the CPC in 1925, emerging as an active organiser in the urban trade union movement during the late 1920s and working closely with Liu Shaoqi. He studied in Moscow in 1927 and between 1935-37; worked in the CPC Organisation Department in the Jiangxi Soviet between 1927-34; took part in the 'Long March' of 1934/5, siding with Mao Zedong at the February 1935 Zunyi Conference; and was elected to the CPC Central Committee in 1934 and Politbureau in 1940. Chen headed the Organisation Department and Rural Works Department at Yanan between 1937-43; chaired the Financial and Economic Committee of the Shaanxi-Gansu-Ningxia border region; and served as Secretary of the CPC's North-eastern (Manchurian) Bureau, where he worked with Gao Gang and Peng Zhen, between 1946-49. Following the CPC's victory in 1949, Chen moved to Peking to serve as a Vice-Premier, being successively concerned with heavy industry, financial affairs and construction. In 1956 he was elected to the Politbureau's Standing Committee and appointed a party Vice-Chairman. During the 'Cultural Revolution' Chen's career retrogressed. Since 1978, however, when he was appointed chairman of the CCID and re-elected to the Politbureau Standing Committee, he has emerged as a central power-broking figure in the Chinese polity.

Chiang Kai-shek (*Jiang Jie Shi* 1887-1975) son of a Zhejiang province village merchant, Chiang trained in Japan, Moscow and at the Huangpu Military Academy at Canton and became the military leader of the Guomindang forces. He became head of the KMT following Sun Zhongshan's death in 1925 and, after the 'Northern Expedition' of 1926/7, broke with the

124

communists in 1927 and proceeded to establish himself as *de jure* ruler of China between 1928-49. Chiang was forced to flee to Taiwan (Formosa) in 1949, following the CPC's conquest of the mainland, and, as head of Taiwan's Republic of China government between 1949-75, continued to claim sovereignty over the Chinese mainland.

COMECON Council for Mutual Economic Assistance. An organisation established in 1949 by the Soviet Union to foster commercial links with its Eastern European satellites. It includes today Bulgaria, Czechoslovakia, Hungary, Poland, Romania, the Soviet Union (all of whom joined in 1949), East Germany (1950), Mongolia (1962), Cuba (1972) and Vietnam (1978).

Communes (*Gongshe*) large collective farming and production units established during the 1950s which have been disbanded in recent years.

Confucius ancient Chinese philosopher, also known as Master Kung (551-479), who visualised the creation of a harmonious new social order based around a virtuous, wise and benevolent ruler enjoying the support of loyal subjects who dutifully performed assigned roles.

CPC Communist Party of China (*Zhongguo Gongchan Dang*)

CPGC Chinese People's Government Council. 1949-54 paramount executive, legislative and judicial body in the PRC.

CPPCC Chinese People's Political Consultative Conference. Broad-front consultative state body.

CPSU Communist Party of the Soviet Union.

Cultural Revolution radical Maoist political and social movement launched in 1966 which sought the removal of politicians who had taken the 'capitalist road', and also the re-emphasis of the primacy of ideology. The 'Cultural Revolution' was at its height between 1966-69, but did not officially end until the death of Mao Zedong and the arrest of the 'Gang of Four' in September-October 1976.

danwei workplace; term given for the assignment of workers to factories for life.

diqu prefecture.

EEC European Economic Community.

Eighth Route Army name given to the CPC forces led by Zhu De and Peng Dehuai at the start of the 1937-45 'Liberation War'.

Five Anti Campaign January-June 1952 rectification movement directed against the urban bourgeoisie, who were accused of bribery, tax avoidance and the thwarting of government regulations.

Four Modernisations programme for rapidly modernising Chinese industry, agriculture, defence and science and technology, first mooted by Zhou Enlai in 1964 and officially introduced in 1975, with the aim of quadrupling per-capita output by the end of the century.

ganbu cadre (party or government official).

Gang of Four radical ultra-leftist grouping of Jiang Qing (Mao Zedong's fourth wife) and three young Shanghai politicians which directed the 'Cultural Revolution' and sought to succeed Mao Zedong in 1976.

GATT General Agreement on Tariffs and Trade; international organisation formed under the auspices of the United Nations in 1947 with the aim of fostering increased international trade through the reduction and removal of tariffs and import quota restrictions.

GNP gross national product; total value of the final goods and services produced in the economy.

Great Leap Forward 1958-60 failed Maoist programme aimed at achieving rapid and simultaneous agricultural and industrial growth and based around the construction of large new agro-industrial communes.

guanxi interpersonal relationships.

Guomindang Chinese Nationalist Party which was established in 1912 and governed much of the country during the interwar period, before being forced to flee to Taiwan (Formosa) in 1949. The party, led by Chiang Ching-kuo (Jiang Jingguo: 1910-), the son of Chiang Kai-shek (Jiang Jie Shi), still claims sovereignty over the Chinese mainland.

Han Chinese term used to designate the Chinese ethnic majority who constitute 94% of the total population.

HEP hydroelectric power.

Huangpu modern military academy (also known as Whampoa) established by Sun Zhongshan at Canton in 1924.

Hundred Flowers Campaign 1956/7 government-encouraged initiative to allow greater artistic and intellectual freedom which was launched with the classical Chinese slogan 'Let a hundred flowers bloom, let the hundred schools of thought contend'. The movement was halted in May 1957, as a result of mounting criticism of the CPC regime, and a harsh anti-rightist campaign instituted.

ICBM inter-continental ballistic missile.

Jiangxi Soviet rural soviet established by Mao Zedong on the Hunan-Jiangxi border between 1931-34.

jingshen wenming spiritual civilisation.

KMT Guomindang Party.

Li Xiannian (*Li Hsien-nien* 1905-) born into a poor Hubei province peasant farming family, Li trained as a carpenter and joined the Guomindang forces during the 'Northern Expedition' of 1926/7, before joining the CPC in 1927. He was a leading figure in the Oyuwan soviet and served as a political commissar during the 1934-36 'Long March' and 1937-45 Liberation War. In 1944 Li was appointed military commander of the Central China military region and in 1949 governor of Hubei. During the 1950s and early 1960s he served as a Vice-Premier and Finance Minister and entered the Politbureau and Secretariat in 1956 and 1958 respectively. Li's career briefly regressed during the 'Cultural Revolution', but he was reappointed Finance Minister in 1973 and was elected to the Politbureau Standing Committee in 1977 and appointed State President in June 1983.

Long March epic 1934-36 movement of CPC forces from soviets in South-central China, besieged by Guomindang forces, to Yanan in Shaanxi province.

luan chaos/disorder.

MAC Military Affairs Commission. The body through which the CPC controls the PLA.

Manchuria (*Dongbei*) the relatively industrialised north-eastern provinces (Liaoning, Jilin and Heilongjiang) of China which were the homelands of the Qing (*Manchu*) emperors and were occupied by Japan in 1931, who set up the puppet regime of Manchukuo nominally headed by the Manchu emperor Puyi.

marshal senior military honour awarded in 1955 to ten military commanders who took part in the 1934-36 'Long March' and 1937-45 Liberation War. Only two marshals, Xu Xiangqian and Nie Rongzhen, remain alive today.

mass line the broad mobilisation of people in economic, social and political movements.

May 4th Movement huge nationalist demonstrations of 4 May 1919 in Peking protesting against the decision of the Versailles Peace Conference to allow Japan to retain German bases in Shandong province seized during the First World War. These bases were returned to China by Japan in 1922.

new model armies Western-style modern armies established by reformers during the late Imperial period.

Northern Expedition successful 1926/7 joint military advance by the KMT and CPC forces from Canton to Wuhan and Shanghai.

NPC National People's Congress (*Quanguo Renmin Diabiao Dahui*), legislature of the PRC.

OPEC Organisation of Petroleum Exporting Countries formed in 1960 to promote the interests of oil-exporting nations by regulating pricing and production.

Oyuwan (or Eyuwan) Soviet rural soviet established on the borders of Hubei, Henan and Anhui provinces by Li Xiannian and Zhang Guohua between 1931-33.

'People's Daily' (*Renmin Ribao*) official daily newspaper of the CPC. Editor (1986) Tan Wenrui; circulation 5 million.

PLA (People's Liberation Army) China's armed forces, including naval and air. Prior to 1946 the PLA was known as the 'Red Army'.

plenum full meeting of the members of a political body.

PPO primary party organisation; bottommost unit of CPC organisation.

PRC People's Republic of China (*Zhonghua Renmin Gongheguo*).

Qing Ming **Festival** traditional Chinese festival held in April for the sweeping of the graves of ancestors. Under the communist regime the festival has been devoted to honouring the 'people's martyrs'.

'Red Flag' (*Hong Qi*) fortnightly theoretical journal of the CPC Central Committee. Editor (1986) Xiong Fu.

Red Guards (*Hong Weibing*) radicalised Maoist students who, with PLA backing, launched the 'Cultural Revolution' attacks against 'rightist' political leaders.

rehabilitation term used for denoting the restoration of a person's political standing or reputation.

responsibility system system of private contracting for production quotas introduced since 1978 which allows farmers to sell surplus production in markets of their choice and to retain the profits.

RMB (*Renminbi*) Chinese 'people's currency' unit (equivalent to £0.19 in 1986).

SAR Special Administrative Region with a high degree of political autonomy which will be formed when Hong Kong and Macao are transferred back to China in 1997 and 1999 respectively.

SCMC State Central Military Commission; body through which the state government monitors the PLA.

SEM Socialist Education Movement; 1962-66 rectification campaign launched by Mao which was designed to remove corruption and to eliminate 'capitalist tendencies' among party cadres. It represented the precursor to the 'Cultural Revolution'.

SEZ Special Economic Zone; a coastal enclave which, since 1979, has been designated for foreign investment through the grant of special tax privileges.

Shan-Tou 'Mountain-top'; Chinese colloquialism for political factions.

Sheng province.

Shi city.

Soviet workers' republic established by the CPC in rural regions during the interwar period.

SPP Supreme People's Procuratorate; the supervisory head of the Chinese legal system.

Te-Quan special privileges of the élite.

thaw term for liberalisation in artistic, ideological and political spheres in communist-controlled regimes.

Third International Comintern the Russian-created communist international movement which functioned between 1919-43 and sought to promote Marxist revolution abroad.

Tienanmen Square square in the centre of Peking outside the former Imperial 'Forbidden City' which is the site of sacred monuments, including the tomb of Mao Zedong. The square, which is adjacent to Zhongnanhai (the compound in which the CPC leadership live and work) and the NPC's Great Hall of the People, has been the scene of many historic rallies and demonstrations.

UN United Nations.

USSR Union of Soviet Socialist Republics (Soviet Union).

xian county.

xiang administrative village or township.

Water Margin (*Shui Hu*) classical Chinese novel concerning a band of rebels who opposed the Imperial Court.

whateverists term given to loyal and unquestioning supporters of Chairman Mao and his writings and thought.

white area KMT Nationalist-controlled area in which CPC activists worked underground during the period after 1927.

work and study intellectuals term give to students who went to France in the years immediately after the First World War on a special programme which combined factory labour and university study.

wuzhi wenming material civilisation.

YCL Young Communist League.

YCP Young Communist Party; Paris branch of the CPC formed in June 1922.

Ye Jianying (*Yeh Chien-ying*: 1896-1986) son of a prosperous Canton trader, Ye joined the CPC in 1927, took part in the 1934-36 'Long March' and served as Chief-of-Staff to the Eighth Route Army during the Liberation War. Ye was appointed governor of the Canton region in 1949, honoured with the rank of marshal in 1955, inducted into the Secretariat in 1966 and replaced Lin Biao as defence minister in 1972. He played a key role in organising the Hua Guofeng coup against the 'Gang of Four' in September-October 1976 and in facilitating the rehabilitation of Deng Xiaoping in 1977. Ye served as chairman of the NPC Standing Committee (and thus as *de facto* head of state) between 1978-83 and as a member of the CPC Politbureau's Standing Committee between 1977-85.

young generals term given to ultra-leftist Red Guard leaders during the 'Cultural Revolution'.

yuan Chinese monetary unit (equivalent to £0.15 in 1987); it is subdivided into 100 fen.

zhengfeng rectification campaign, which, following the precepts of Maoist and Confucianist teachings, aims at the re-education of misguided individuals.

zhiren zhi 'contract' or 'responsibility system' recently introduced into the rural sector.

zhou autonomous area.

Zhu De (*Chu-teh* 1886-1976) son of a wealthy Sichuan province landlord, Zhu initially served in the Chinese Imperial Army, but sided with Sun Zhongshan in the 1911 Revolution. After studying communism in Germany and Paris during the early 1920s, he joined the CPC in 1925 and worked with Mao Zedong at the Jiangxi soviet, helping to devise the new tactics of guerrilla warfare and commanding the CPC's forces in the 'Long March' of 1934-36 and Liberation Struggle and Civil War of 1937-49. He was appointed a marshal in 1955 and served as a senior member of the Politbureau and MAC in the new PRC and as Chairman of the NPC Standing Committee (i.e. as head of state) between 1975/6.

Zunyi town in Guizhou province where, during the 'Long March', Mao Zedong was elected CPC chairman at a special conference in February 1935.

RECENT BOOKS ON CHINESE POLITICS

R. BAUM (Ed) *China's Four Modernizations*: The New Technical Revolution (Boulder, Col.: Westview Press 1980)

G. BENNETT *Huadong*: The Story of a Chinese People's Commune (Boulder, Col.: Westview Press 1978)

G. BENTON (Ed) *Wild Lilies, Poisonous Weeds*: Dissident Voices from the People's China (London: Pluto Press 1982)

D. BLOODWORTH *The Messiah and the Mandarins*: The Paradox of Mao's China (London: Weidenfeld and Nicolson 1982)

D. BONAVIA *The Chinese*: A Portrait (London: Allen Lane 1980)

D. BONAVIA *Verdict in Peking*: The Trial of the Gang of Four (London: Burnett 1984)

J. BREDSDORFF *Revolution*: There and Back (London: Faber 1980)

B. BRUGGER (Ed) *China Since the Gang of Four* (London: Croom Helm 1980)

B. BRUGGER *China*: Liberation and Transformation, 1942-1962 (London: Croom Helm 1981)

B. BRUGGER *China* Radicalism to Revisionism, 1962-1979 (London: Croom Helm 1981)

F. M. BUNGE & R. S. SHINN *China*: A Country Study (Washington DC: The American University 1981)

A. CHAN *Children of Mao* (London: Macmillan 1985)

F. P. F. CHAN *The People's Republic of China*: Modernisation and Legal Development (London: Longman, 2nd Edn 1983)

D. W. CHANG *Zhou Enlai and Deng Xiaoping in the Chinese Leadership Succession Crisis* (London: University Press of America 1984)

P. H. CHANG *Power and Policy in China* (London: Pennsylvania State University Press 1978)

J. CHEN *Inside the Cultural Revolution* (London: Sheldon Press 1976)

J. F. COOPER *China's Global Role*: An Analysis of Peking's National Power Capability in the Context of an Evolving International System (Stanford University: Hoover Institute 1980)

DENG XIAOPING *Speeches and Writings* (Oxford: Pergamon 1984)

J. DOMES *China after the Cultural Revolution*: Politics Between Two Party Congresses (Berkeley: University of California Press 1977)

J. DOMES (Ed) *Chinese Politics After Mao* (Cardiff: Cardiff University Press 1979)

J. DOMES *Peng Te-huai*: The Man and the Image (London: C. Hurst and Co. 1985)

A. ECKSTEIN *China's Economic Revolution* (Cambridge: Cambridge University Press 1977)

L. FEIGON *Chen Duxiu*: Founder of the Chinese Communist Party (Princeton, New Jersey: Princeton University Press 1983)

J. K. FAIRBANK *The Great Chinese Revolution, 1800-1985* (London: Chatto and Windus 1987)

C. P. FITZGERALD *Mao Tse-tung and China* (Harmondsworth: Penguin 1977)

J. FRASER *The Chinese*: Portrait of a People (London: Collins 1981)

J. GARDNER *Chinese Politics and the Succession to Mao* (London: Macmillan 1982)

R. GARSIDE *Coming Alive!*: China after Mao (London: Andre Deutsch 1981)

M. GOLDMAN *China's Intellectuals*: Advise and Dissent (Cambridge, Mass.: Harvard University Press 1981)

J. GUILLERMAZ *The Chinese Communist Party in Power, 1949-1974* (Boulder, Col.: Westview Press 1976)

WENG GUNGWU *China and the World Since 1949*: The Impact of Independence, Modernity and Revolution (London: Macmillan 1977)

J. G. BURLEY *China's Economy and the Maoist Strategy* (London: Monthly Review Press 1976)

H. HARDING *Organising China*: The Problems of Bureaucracy, 1949-1976 (Stanford: Stanford University Press 1981)

H. HARDING (Ed) *China's Foreign Relations in the 1980s* (New Haven: Yale University Press 1984)

P. HARRIS *Political China Observed*: A Western Perspective (London: Croom Helm 1980)

LIANG HENG & J. SHAPIRO *Cold Winds, Warm Winds*: Intellectuals in China (London: Harper and Row 1986)

LIANG HENG & J. SHAPIRO *Return to China* (London: Chatto 1986)

H. C. HINTON *An Introduction to Chinese Politics* (New York: Praeger 1978)

H. C. HINTON (Ed) *The People's Republic of China*: A Handbook (Folkestone: Dawson 1979)

C. HOLLINGSWORTH *Mao and the Men Against Him* (London: Jonathan Cape 1985)

R. HOWARD *Mao Tse-tung and the Chinese People* (London: Allen and Unwin 1977)

J. P. JAIN *After Mao What?*: Army, Party and Group Rivalries in China (London: Martin Robertson 1976)

H. KAPUR *The End of Isolation*: China after Mao (Dordrecht: Martinus Nijhoff 1985)

S. KARNOW *Mao and China*: Inside the Chinese Cultural Revolution (Harmondsworth: Penguin 1984)

N. KOLPAS *Mao* (Harlow: Longman 1981)

W. KRAUS *Economic Development and Social Change in the People's Republic of China* (New York: Springer-Verlag 1979)

CHING HUA LEE *Deng Xiaoping*: The Marxist Road to the Forbidden City (Princeton: Kingston Press 1985)

HONG YUNG LEE *The Politics of the Chinese Cultural Revolution* (Berkeley: University of California Press 1978)

S. LEYS *The Chairman's New Clothes*: Mao and the Cultural Revolution (London: Allison and Busby 1981)

R. MACFARQUHAR *The Origins of the Cultural Revolution*, Vol II: The Great Leap Forward (New York: Columbia University Press 1983)

N. MAXWELL & B. McFARLANE (Eds) *China's Road to Development* (Oxford: Pergamon 1984)

R. MEDVEDEV *China and the Superpowers* (Oxford: Basil Blackwell 1986)

P. R. MOODY *Opposition and Dissent in Contemporary China* (Stanford: Hoover Institute 1977)

A. J. NATHAN *Chinese Democracy*: The Individual and the State in Twentieth Century China (London: I. B. Taurus 1986)

H. W. NELSEN *The Chinese Military System*: An Organizational Study of the Chinese People's Liberation Army (Boulder, Col.: Westview Press 1977)

A. D. ONATE *Chairman Mao and the Chinese Communist Party* (Chicago: Nelson Hall 1979)

F. K. POOLE *Mao* (London: Watts 1984)

J. POSADAS *China* (London: Scientific, Cultural and Political Education 1981)

L. PYE *The Dynamics of Chinese Politics* (Cambridge, Mass.: Delgeschlager, Gunn & Hain 1981)

S. ROSEN *Red Guard Factionalism and the Cultural Revolution in Guangzhou* (Boulder, Col.: Westview Press 1982)

W. G. ROSENBERG & M. B. YOUNG *Transforming Russia and China* (Oxford: Oxford University Press 1982)

T. SAICH *China*: Politics and Government (London: Macmillan 1981)

H. E. SALISBURY *The Long March* (London: Macmillan 1985)

O. SCHELL *To Get Rich is Glorious*: China in the Eighties (London: Robin Clark Ltd 1985)

S. R. SCHRAM *Ideology and Policy in China since the 3rd Plenum, 1978-84* (London: University of London 1984)

G. SEGAL *The Great Power Triangle* (London: Macmillan 1981)

G. SEGAL *Defending China* (Oxford: Oxford University Press 1985)

D. L. SHAMBAUGH *The Making of a Premier*: Zhao Ziyang's Provincial Career (Epping: Bowker 1984)

P. SHORT *The Dragon and the Bear* (London: Hodder & Stoughton 1982)

V. SHUE *Peasant China in Transition* (Berkeley: University of California Press 1980)

PEY SHU-TSE *The Chinese Communist Party in Power* (New York: Monad Press 1980)

B. SMITH *Mao's Last Battle*: The Next Stage (London: China Policy Group 1978)

H. SUYIN *Wind in the Tower*: Mao Tse-tung and the Chinese Revolution, 1949-76 (London: Jonathan Cape 1976)

F. C. TEIWES *Politics and Purges in China*: Rectification and the Decline of Party Norms, 1950-1965 (White Plains: M. E. Sharpe 1979)

F. C. TEIWES *Leadership, Legitimacy and Conflict in China*: From a

Charismatic Mao to the Politics of Succession (London: Macmillan 1984)

R. TERRILL (Ed) *The China Difference* (London: Harper and Row 1979)

R. TERRILL *The Future of China after Mao* (New York: Delacorte Press 1978)

R. TERRILL *Mao*: A Biography (London: Harper and Row 1980)

R. TERRILL *The White Boned Demon*: A Biography of Madame Mao Zedong (London: Heinemann 1984)

J. R. TOWNSEND *Politics in China* (Toronto: Little, Brown & Co 1980)

E. VOGEL *Canton Under Communism* (Cambridge, Mass.: Harvard University Press, 2nd Edn 1980)

D. J. WALLER *The Government and Politics of the People's Republic of China* (London: Hutchinson, 3rd Edn 1981)

J. C. F. WANG *Contemporary Chinese Politics*: An Introduction (London: Prentice Hall 1980)

TING WANG *Chairman Hua*: The Leader of the Chinese Communists (London: C. Hurst and Co 1980)

A. S. WHITING *Chinese Domestic Politics and Foreign Policy in the 1970s* (Michigan University Press 1979)

D. WILSON (Ed) *Mao Tse-tung in the Scales of History* (Cambridge: Cambridge University Press 1978)

D. WILSON *Mao*: The People's Emperor (London: Futura 1980)

D. WILSON *Chou*: The Story of Zhou Enlai, 1898-1976 (London: Hutchinson 1984)

R. WITKE *Comrade Chiang Ch'ing* (London: Weidenfeld and Nicolson 1977)

P. WONG *China's Higher Leadership in the Socialist Transition* (London: Collier Macmillan 1976)

TIEN-WEI WU *Lin Biao and the Gang of Four*: Contra-Confucianism in Historical and Intellectual Perspective (Carbondale: Southern Illinois University Press 1983)

M. B. YAHUDA *China's Role in World Affairs* (London: Croom Helm 1978)

M. YAO *The Conspiracy and Death of Lin Biao* (New York: A. A. Knopf 1983)

KWAN HA YIM (Ed) *China Since Mao* (New York: Facts on File 1980)

CHRONOLOGY OF RECENT EVENTS: 1973-1987

1973 Aug: 10th CPC Congress; 'Criticise Confucius' campaign.

1974 April: Deng's 'Three Worlds' speech at UN.

1975 Jan: 4th NPC Congress adopts new State constitution, launches 'Four Modernisations. Sept: *Water Margin* campaign.

1976 Jan: Zhou Enlai dies. Feb: Hua Guofeng appointed acting Premier. April: Tienanmen Square demonstrations, Deng dismissed from leadership posts. Sept: Mao Zedong dies, Hua elected CPC Chairman. Oct: 'Gang of Four' arrested.

1977 July: Deng exonerated and restored to office. Aug: 11th CPC Congress — further 'Dengists' rehabilitated.

1978 Feb-March: 5th NPC Congress — Ye Jianying elected Head of State, new State constitution adopted; CPPCC revived. Dec: 3rd Plenum of 11th CPC Central Committee establishes Deng in power and approves economic reform programme; 'Democracy Wall' campaign; diplomatic relations with United States formalised.

1979 Jan: Deng visits Washington.; Feb: crackdown against 'Democracy Wall' dissidents; China-Vietnam 14-day war. June: NPC adopts new constitutional laws. Dec: USSR invades Afghanistan.

1980 Feb: purge of 'whateverist' clique from Politbureau; Hu Yaobang appointed CPC General-Secretary. Aug-Sept: Zhao Ziyang replaces Hua as Premier. Nov: trial of 'Gang of Four' begins.

1981 Jan: 'Gang of Four' found guilty; President Reagan enters White House. June: Hu Yaobang replaces Hua as CPC Chairman.

1982 Sept: 12th CPC Congress — new party constitution, creates CAC and abolishes chairmanship; Hua ousted from Politbureau. Dec: new State constitution, creates SCMC and post of President.

1983 June: 6th NPC — Li Xiannian elected State President; party rectification campaign launched.

1984 Oct: urban reform programme introduced. Dec: Hong Kong accord.

1985 March: Gorbachev assumes Soviet leadership. June: infusion of new technocrat State Ministers. July: PLA reorganisation. Sept-Oct: 131 resignations from Politbureau and Central Committee; Special Party Conference; promotion of '3rd Echelon' into Politbureau and Central Committee.

1986 Jan: new party anti-corruption and reform campaign. June: commencement of cultural thaw. Oct: deaths of Marshals Ye Jianying and Liu Bocheng. Dec: student democracy movement in the provinces and Peking.

1987 Jan: crackdown against democracy movement; replacement of Hu Yaobang by Zhao Ziyang as CPC General-Secretary. Feb: launch of conservative anti-bourgeois liberalism campaign.